MW01109741

Biad Chili Tough Book of Green Chile Recipes

www.BiadChili.com
www.facebook.com/HatchGreenChile

Published by Family Cookbook Project, LLC
PO Box 262 W Simsbury CT 06092 (printed in Canada)

CookbookFundraiser.com - create a successful fundraiser!
Visit us on the Web at
www.CookbookFundraiser.com

Foreword

When "NMSU Aggies Are Tough Enough to Wear Pink" was created in 2007, no one could have imagined what it would become six years later. Every year another generous Las Cruces or southern New Mexico business finds a new, creative and innovative way to make a significant contribution to the breast cancer research fundraising and awareness work to which we're committed.

This cookbook is the brainchild of our friends at Biad Chili Products. For their generous participation in the 2012 TETWP campaign, we offer our sincere gratitude and heartfelt appreciation. The cookbook itself is full of wonderful recipes, but it represents much more than a collection of tasty treats. It is representative of forward thinking, community minded businesses that has helped us raise more than $2 million dollars in cash and in-kind contributions for Cowboys for Cancer Research.

The TETWP co-chairs and our entire volunteer committee thank Biad Chili Products for this amazing publication. We wish you many happy meals!

Pat Sisbarro, Laura Conniff, Mary Henson, Magellia Boston

Preface

Cancer has touched all of our lives in one way or another. For us at Biad Chili, cancer has affected our family members and employees. It is our desire that this cookbook will be a link in the chain to raise awareness and funds to fight cancer. We would like to thank everyone who submitted their recipes for the contest and give a special thanks to our judge Chef Maurice Zeck. We hope that you enjoy this cookbook and we thank you for your support!

-Biad Chili Products.

Contributors

Aaron Bensonhaver (Florida)

Aaron Hill (California)

Alice Shaul Ririe (Oklahoma)

Amanda Green (Alabama)

Ann Walsh (North Carolina)

Arnold Montoya (New Mexico)

Barbara Rose Farber (New Mexico)

Bernadette Michelle Morales (California)

Beth Stephens (New Mexico)

Betty Brooks (New Mexico)

Brian Rose (California)

Bryan Benham (Colorado)

Carter White (California)

Cathleen Krepps (New Mexico)

Christina Segura (California)

Dana Wagenhoffer (New Mexico)

Dava Beck (Oklahoma)

David Leong (New Mexico)

Debbie Ferreira (New Mexico)

Debbie Smith (Texas)

DeLoris Scherschligt (Oregon)

Don Shows (New Mexico)

Eddie Dehart (New Mexico)

Elaine Gonzalez (Arizona)

Erin Hurt (Texas)

Frances Vigil (New Mexico)

Greg Courtney (Texas)

Henry Lombrana (Texas)

Ian J. B. Kelley (Colorado)

Jeff Hornstein (New Mexico)

Jerry Lisby (Texas)

Jim Arnold (Texas)

John Humphreys (Idaho)

Jordan Calaway (California)

Joyce Sizemore (Georgia)

Judy Toledo Lopez (California)

Kathy Mondragon (New Mexico)

Kenn E. Ashe (New Mexico)

Kim Powell (Georgia)

Kim Smith Casford (New Mexico)

Laura Hall (Washington)

Laurel Marshall (Nevada)

Laurie Smith (New Mexico)

Lorale McConley (Colorado)

Maria Ifill (New Mexico)

Maria Rocha (New Mexico)

Marie Gherghei (Ohio)

Marie Perucca-Ramirez (California)

Martha Grose (Missouri)

Matt Brooks (Washington)

Michael McGinness (Missouri)

Mike (Wyoming)

Pat Hill (New Mexico)

Patrick Driscoll (Arizona)

Paul Kmetko (California)

Rachel Johnson (New Mexico)

Rebecca Allen (California)

Robert Pirtle (New Mexico)

Russell Stone (Wisconsin)

Sara Anderson (Colorado)

Sonia Rabara (Texas)

Susan Hershberger (Arizona)

Tamara Dixon (Washington)

Tishia Stewart (New Mexico)

Wendi McClaren-Geis (Colorado)

Peggy A. Nelson (New Mexico)

Randall Stwalley (Colorado)

Rebecca Rivera (Louisiana)

Russell Blundell (New Mexico)

Sandi Lanning (New Mexico)

Shawna Blair (Colorado)

Steve Hach (Pennsylvania)

Tamar Sisneros (Washington)

Terri Thompson (New Mexico)

Todd Lund (Texas)

Table of Contents

Appetizers

SPICE GUIDE

Keep spices in tightly covered containers, in a cool dry place. After about a year, spices tend to lose flavor so more may be needed for seasonings. Overheating can cause spices to turn bitter. During lengthy cooking, add spices during the last half hour of cooking time. Usually 1 teaspoon of dried herb equals 1 tablespoon of fresh.

ALLSPICE: *Flavor a blend of cinnamon, cloves and nutmeg.* Meat dishes, egg dishes, fish, gravies, pickles, relishes, tomato sauce, fruit preserves.

BASIL: *Pungent, sweet aroma.* Broiled and roasted meats and poultry, fish, egg dishes, soups, vegetables, tomato dishes, pasta, dressings, sauces.

BAY LEAF: *Strong flavor.* Stews, soups, vegetables, pickles, gravies, sauces, marinades.

CAYENNE: *Red pepper, very hot.* Meats, seafoods, egg and cheese dishes, soups, sauces, dips, spreads, French dressing.

CHILI POWDER: *Hot, peppery blend of herbs and spices.* Spanish or Mexican dishes, bean and rice dishes, barbeque and cocktail sauces, spreads, dressings, dips, egg dishes, vegetables.

CINNAMON: *Sweet, spicy aroma.* Breads, cookies, cakes, desserts, pastries, beverages, sauces, vegetables.

CLOVES: *Strong, spicy-sweet aroma.* Pork and lamb dishes, barbeque sauce, pickles, relishes, fruits, breads, cakes, cookies, desserts.

CUMIN: *Strong, slightly bitter, lemon flavor.* Spanish, Mexican and Eastern dishes, stews, pickles, tomato dishes.

CURRY: *A blend of many spices; warm and sharp to hot and spicy.* Meat, seafood, egg and cheese dishes, soups, sauces, seafood, salads, dips.

DILL SEED: *Mild, slight caraway-like flavor.* Meats, poultry, fish, seafood, stews, soups, salads, sauces, dressings, dips, pickles, breads, egg dishes.

GINGER: *Pleasant odor, pungent taste.* Oriental dishes, meats, vegetables, fruits, salad dressings, pickles, jams, marinades, breads, desserts.

MARJORAM: *Spicy, sweet aroma.* Roasted meats and poultry, fish and seafood, egg dishes, stews and casseroles, soups, vegetables, salads, gravies.

MUSTARD: *Pungent taste.* Pickles, relishes, salad dressings, sauces, dips, egg dishes, marinades, pork and ham, corned beef.

NUTMEG: *Warm, sweet, spicy flavor.* Vegetables, egg dishes, beverages, breads, cookies, cakes, desserts, sauces.

OREGANO: *Strong and aromatic.* Italian dishes, pizza and pasta, broiled and roasted meats, fish and seafood, stews and casseroles, egg dishes, tomato sauces, soups, vegetables, salads, salad dressings.

PAPRIKA: *Varies from mild, slightly sweet to hot; adds colour to many dishes.* Meats, poultry, salad dressings, dips, vegetables, soups and salads.

PARSLEY: *Mild flavor.* Brings out the flavor of most non-sweet foods.

ROSEMARY: *Sweet, spicy, pine-like fragrance.* Roasted meat and poultry, fish, stews, casseroles, stuffings, salads, breads, egg dishes.

SAGE: *Strong, slightly bitter.* Roasted meats and poultry, fish, stuffings, vegetables, cheese dishes, salads, gravies, sauces.

New Mexico Guacamole

Tamara Dixon (Washington)

Green chile (2 full chilies)
Avocado (3 medium)
Tomato (1 small)

Cilantro (a few sprigs)
Garlic salt (to taste)

Peel and mash avocados, saving 1 seed for later. Chop tomato and cilantro then combine all ingredients and mix. Add garlic salt to taste. Include seed in mix to keep dip from turning brown.

Best Bean Dip Ever

Judy Toledo Lopez (California)

1 can of re-fried black beans
1 can of whole black beans
1 cup extra sharp cheddar cheese

4 oz cream cheese
1 small diced onion
1/2 cup roasted extra hot chopped green chile

In a bowl, blend all the ingredients together. Heat in either a microwave or an oven until both cheeses are melted. Serve warm with tortilla chips.

Creamy Hatch Green Chile Ranch Dip

Todd Lund (Texas)

4 fire roasted Hatch green chiles -
deseeded and chopped
1/4 cup of fresh chopped cilantro
1 packet Hidden Valley Ranch
dressing

1 cup Olive Oil Mayo
1 cup Buttermilk
1 fresh lime

De-seed and chop hatch chilies. Remove stems and chop cilantro. Add all ingredients into food processor. Squeeze the juice from one half of lime into processor. Mix thoroughly. Refrigerate before serving. Great for dipping chips, and using as sauce.

Green Chili poppers

Bernadette Michelle Morales (California)

1 lb ground beef
I/4 cup onion
3 eggs
1/2 cup flour
2 cups oil

1/2tsp salt and pepper
1/2 cup green chili chopped
1/2 tsp thyme
1/2 tsp ground cumin
1/2 tsp lemon juice

Blend ground beef, chili, salt, pepper, one egg in a bowl.
Roll into bite sizes balls or press into coins.
Mix flour, thyme, and cumin
Beat egg and lemon
Roll meatballs in flour, then dip in egg and roll in flour again.
Deep fry till golden brown, place on paper towel. Enjoy! Use ranch on the side if wanted.

Green Chile Avocado Salsa

Sandi Lanning (New Mexico)

8 roasted, peeled & chopped green
  chiles (you choose the heat)
3 ripe, (but not mushy) chopped
  avocados
1 small red onion (about 1/2 c
  chopped)
2 cloves garlic (minced)
2 plum tomatoes (chopped)
2 tomatillos (chopped)

1 TBS Cumin
1/4 cup chopped fresh cilantro (1 TBS
  dried)
1 tsp salt
1 tsp pepper
juice of 1/2 lime
1/4 cup olive oil

In a large bowl add the chile, onion, garlic, avocado, tomatillos, and tomatoes. Add the lime juice and spices mix lightly.
Finally, add the olive oil and mix until distributed evenly. Serve with warm tortilla chips.

ChaCha's Chile Con Queso

Sonia Rabara (Texas)

7-9 Hatch roasted, peeled, chopped
  chiles (half hot and half mild)
1 onion diced very fine
2 medium tomatoes
1 can tomato sauce
1/2 lbs to 1 pound of Monterrey
  cheese

1 cup water
2 tablespoons oil
1 tablespoon Salt
1 tablespoon Powdered Garlic

Heat pan with oil until hot.
Add onions and chopped chile.
Saute for a few minutes
Then add tomatoes, pour in cup of water
Add Salt and Garlic powder,
Add tomato sauce until you bring to a boil. Turn Heat off.
At the end, add your chunks of cheese until it melts....

Your mouth will water, not only will it taste delicious with tostadas, you can add it on top of your favorite dishes.

Matt's Green Chile Goat Cheese Quesadillas

Matt Brooks (Washington)

4 large flour tortillas
6 oz goat cheese, at room temperature
1/2 cup chopped green chile, well
  drained

1 handful fresh cilantro, coarsely
  chopped
olive oil

To make ONE quesadilla: lightly brush one side of a tortilla with olive oil, and place oil-side down in a heavy skillet on medium-warm. Place chunks of goat cheese on the tortilla - the larger the chunks, the better. When the cheese begins to soften, add about 3 tablespoons of green chile and two or three generous pinches of cilantro. When the tortilla begins to brown in spots, according to taste, remove from the skillet, fold in half. and cut into three wedges. Repeat with remaining tortillas. Excellent as an appetizer or as a light main course for lunch.

Hatcha Batcha Green Chile Dip

Aaron Hill (California)

4 grilled or pan sauteed chicken breasts
3/4 cup pepper sauce (Cholula, Tabasco or Frank's Red Hot depending on what you like)
2 (8 ounce) packages cream cheese, softened
1 cup Blue Cheese or Ranch dressing
2 cups shredded Cheddar cheese

1 13 oz container of your favorite chopped Biad Green Chiiles

1 bunch celery, cleaned and cut into 4 inch pieces
1 bag good quality tortilla chips

Grill or pan saute chicken breast. Dice chicken breast into small pieces and combine with hot sauce in a skillet over medium heat. Stir in cream cheese and blue cheese/ranch dressing. Cook, stirring until well blended and warm. Mix in half of the shredded cheese and green chilies, and transfer the mixture to a casserole pan. Sprinkle the remaining cheese over the top, cover, and cook at 350 until hot and bubbly and cheese is browned (about 25 minutes). Serve with celery sticks and tortilla chips.

Mama C's Flaming Salsa

Christina Segura (California)

2 lbs Pork cushion meat
1 medium whole onion
6 roasted tomatoes
4 garlic cloves smashed (pressed)
1 tsp cumin
salt and pepper to taste

1 pinch of fresh oregano
1 tsp sugar
3 tsp manteca
2 lbs fresh Nopales (washed and sliced)
12 large roasted hot New Mexico hatch chiles
6 cups water

In large dutch oven cook cushion meat for 1-1/2 hours on medium heat. Add salt, pepper, cumin, oregano and cook until meat is tender and falls apart, then set aside. Save the broth. On stove top roast tomatoes on high flame till skin is blackened, then peel off skin.
In large skillet (preferably cast iron) add manteca. When hot add

thinly sliced onion and garlic till roasted. Add pork and fry till nice and roasted. In dutch oven with the broth add tomatoes, nopales and the pork mixture. Cook on medium for 30 minuets then add chopped green chile and sugar. Cook another 30 minutes till nice and thick. Goes great with about anything. Enjoy!

Mini Green Chile Stew Spring Rolls (Top 10 Grand Prize Winner)

Jerry Lisby (Texas)

1/2 lb pork loin, diced (small 1/4 inch)
1/4 C Flour
1 Tbsp NM red chile
2 Tbsp Vegetable oil
1 Tbsp bacon grease
2 Tsp Fresh ground pepper
1 C Onion chopped fine
3 Garlic cloves, minced
1 C Chopped Hatch Green Chile

1 C Low sodium chicken broth

2 Tsp salt
1 C Potato diced (small ¼ inch)

1 Pkg mini spring roll wrappers
1 Egg white
Vegetable oil for frying

• Mix flour and NM red chile powder
• Dredge pork in flour... shake off excess flour
• On med-high heat in a nonstick frying pan heat oil and bacon grease, brown pork with onion until pork is lightly browned 2-3 min
• Add garlic and green chile stir for 1-2 minutes
• Transfer to a 2 qt sauce pan
• Add chicken broth and fresh ground pepper
• Cover and simmer on low heat for at least ½ hour, stirring occasionally
• Add potato and simmer until potatoes are cooked through
• Cool stew for 2-3 hours or overnight
• Place 1 tbsp of cooled stew in mini spring roll wrapper (use two wrappers) seal edges with egg white
• Fry in Vegetable oil at 375 degrees 3-4 minutes or until golden brown

Balloon Greg's Green Chile Roll-Ups

Greg Courtney (Texas)

2 16 oz. cream cheese (you can use low fat, but regular turns out much better).
1 white onion, finely minced.
1 red onion, finely minced.
2 large (or 4 small) bunches of green onions, finely minced (including green parts).
1 1/2 teaspoons finely minced garlic.

1 to 1 1/2 cups green chile, finely minced (because of the cream cheese, you can use a hotter chile than you usually would).
1 teaspoon cumin.
several "splashes" of Tabasco or Chipotle Tabasco sauce.
A couple of packages of 12 inch, thin flour tortillas. You can be creative during the holidays and get different colors (flavors) of tortillas.
salt and white pepper if desired.

Warm cream cheese until soft. Mix all ingredients together until well blended. Spread thinly on the tortillas. Roll the tortillas up, wrap them in plastic wrap and refrigerate (overnight if possible because the flavors meld together). When cool and firm, cut each roll into slices, garnish with cilantro.

This is an hors d'oeuvre that you cannot make enough of. I have taken them to the office and within minutes each person had consumed more than a dozen. I, myself, cannot eat just a few.

Makes several dozen depending on how thick you slice them. They freeze well.

Hatch Green Chili Mexican Queso

Shawna Blair (Colorado)

3 Tbsp Olive Oil
1 Large Onion Chopped
6 Jalapeños Sliced in Rounds
1 Tbsp Mexican Oregano
1 1/2 to 2 cups Chicken Stock

1 Large Can Tomatillo Tomatoes
1 14.5 oz. can Stewed Tomatoes
2 Cups Hatch Green Chile (roasted, peeled, & chopped)
1 lb. Oaxaca Cheese cubed (Monterey Jack can be substituted)

In a large chili pot, add Olive Oil and bring to medium

temperature. Add chopped onion, oregano and jalapeños, saute for 5 minutes or until onions are translucent.

Add Tomatillos and Stewed Tomatoes, bring pot to a simmer for 15 minutes.

Add Hatch Chopped Green Chile, bring pot to a simmer for another 15 minutes and slowly add the cubed cheese and keep stirring until all the cheese is blended. Add more or less cheese to your liking.

Serve right out of the pot into soup bowls for a family appetizer or meal in itself.

Transfer from chili pot to a preheated crock pot on medium to serve at a party and provide bowls and spoons.

Serve with Tostada Chips and/or flour or corn tortillas.

When reheating, add more chicken stock.

Personal Notes: Select the level of hotness in the chilies that is appropriate for your liking. I suggest a mix of medium and hot together to blend both awesome flavors without burning your intestines the next day! ;)

Green Chile Relleno Taquitos with Avocado-Tomatillo Salsa

Jeff Hornstein (New Mexico)

Taquitos:
- 6 medium-heat (or to taste) roasted, skinned and seeded green chiles
- 1 cup soft goat cheese or Mexican queso fresco
- 1 very firm medium tomato finely diced
- 1 small onion finely chopped -three sprigs cilantro finely chopped
- 1 large clove garlic finely chopped
- 6 large THIN flower tortillas
- 1 quarter cup vegetable oil (corn or canola work well)

The Salsa:
- 3 roasted or boiled medium tomatillos (green tomatoes) (allow the tomatillos to cool before mixing the salsa)
- 1 large soft avocado
- the juice from three small limes
- 1 large pinch each sea salt
- 1 pinch sugar
- 1 pinch oregano

The Taquitos:
Mix the cheese, onion, tomato, garlic and cilantro until combined.

Generously stuff the green chilies with the cheese mixture. (the chilies should be patted dry with a paper towel)

Tightly roll the stuffed chiles in the tortillas burrito style with the ends folded in. (the tortillas can be steamed or microwaved if they aren't easily foldable) Use Toothpicks to secure the rolled taquitos.

Fry the taquitos in the oil in a shallow pan until they are golden brown. Pat the excess oil off with a paper towel.

The Salsa:
Put all of the salsa ingredients in a blender or food processor and mix until you have a creamy consistency.

Serve warm with the salsa drizzled over the taquitos or with the salsa in a dish for dipping.

Soups

MICROWAVE COOKING HINTS

To speed cooking and promote even heating, use the following techniques:

- Stir food during cooking to bring the heated outside parts to the centre.

- Turn food over when microwaving small items like hamburgers or chops, or when defrosting.

- Rearrange foods or individual items during cooking to promote even heating.

- Allow standing time to complete the cooking of roasts and baked products.

- Shield wings or legs of poultry with small pieces of aluminum foil to prevent over-cooking of these parts.

- Cover foods to hold in moisture and speed cooking.

- Arrange foods in a ring or circular shape to allow maximum exposure to microwave energy. Place tender or thin parts in the centre and thicker pieces toward the outside.

- Rotate or move food a quarter or half turn during cooking to allow foods which cook quickly to cook evenly.

- Select foods or pieces of the same size and shape because small items cook faster than large ones.

- Food at refrigerator temperature takes longer to cook than food at room temperature.

- Dense foods take more time to heat than light or porous foods.

Green Chile Chicken Cheese Soup

Russell Blundell (New Mexico)

1/2 cup Green Chile
1 cup Chicken
1 small Onion
4 cloves garlic
2 tablespoon flour
1 1/2-2 cups small red potatoes
6 cups heavy whipping cream

1 tablespoon thyme
1 tablespoon Oregano
2 cups Mozzarella Cheese
1 Cup Parmesan Cheese
1/4 cup olive oil
2 tablespoon salt

In a large pan caramelize diced onion and diced garlic in olive oil. Add flour to thicken. Add diced potatoes (~1/2 squares) green chile, spices and whipping cream then bring to almost a boil, turn down heat and continue to cook until potatoes are soft without falling apart. Add both cheese gradually, continue to cook until cheese is melted completely. Turn off heat and let set for at least 30 minutes, then serve. Try not to eat it all in one serving.

Green Chile Corn Chowder

Terri Thompson (New Mexico)

Can of creamed corn
2-3 tsp olive oil
4-5 roasted green chilies, diced
1/2 yellow onion, diced
3 cloves garlic, minced

2 medium potatoes, peeled and diced
24 oz chicken or vegetable broth
8 oz sour cream
8 oz shredded cheddar cheese
homemade flour tortillas

Saute the garlic and onion in olive oil in a dutch oven pot for about 5 min until translucent, add all remaining ingredients except for sour cream and cheese. Cover and simmer until the potatoes are cooked (about 30-45 min depending on how thin they are). To thicken the soup, use a hand blender to partially blend the vegetables to your liking. Serve steaming hot in bowls with a scoop of sour cream and some shredded cheese, and a warm tortilla.

Green Chile Bacon Corn Chowder Goodness (Top 10 Grand Prize Winner)

Kim Powell (Georgia)

5 slices bacon, chopped
1 large onion, minced
3 cups frozen corn kernels
3 cups whole milk
1 pound red potatoes, peeled and diced

1 teaspoon salt
1/2 cup whipping cream
1 cup roasted, peeled and chopped medium or hot green New Mexican Chilies
2 tablespoons fresh chives, minced

Fry the bacon in a large saucepan over medium heat until brown and crisp.
Remove the bacon with a slotted spoon and put aside. Stir the onion into the bacon drippings and cook until the onion is soft and clear- about 5 minutes.
Puree 1 cup of corn with 1 cup of milk in a blender. Pour the mixture into the pan and add the remaining milk and corn along with the potatoes and 1 teaspoon of salt. Reduce the heat to medium-low and cook 10 to 15 minutes, or until the potatoes are fork-tender. Stir in the cream and the green chile. Add salt and pepper, to taste. Ladle the chowder into bowls, garnish with chives and the reserved bacon, and serve.
Serve with warm bread.
Ooooh Yum!!!

Green Chile, Chicken Lime Soup

Brian Rose (California)

3 Chicken Breasts, grilled and shredded
6 Roasted Green Chilies
1 medium onion
3 cloves garlic
2 tsp. cumin
1-28 oz can cubed tomatoes

1-28 oz can hominy
Juice of three limes
Water
Salt to taste
Fresh Cilantro as garnish
Tortilla strips as garnish

Grill Chicken, preferably over mesquite charcoal until done. Cool and shred.

Dice onion into small cubes.

Mince garlic finely

Roast Chilies (also over mesquite) until tender, allow to cool and chop into 1/4" or smaller pieces.

Add all ingredients other than the lime juice to 5 quart soup pan. Add water to cover ingredients. Bring to a boil and reduce to simmer. Cook over low heat for 2-3 hours adding salt as needed for personal taste. If soup becomes too thick, add additional water. Should be a thick consistency soup when finished.

Just before removing from heat, add juice of the limes.

Garnish bowl with fresh cilantro leaves and tortilla strips.

Serve hot and enjoy

Green Chile Soup

Dava Beck (Oklahoma)

1 tablespoon vegetable oil
1 cup chopped onion
1 cup chopped red bell pepper
3 cloves garlic, minced
2 lb. pork steak, cut into cubes
2 cans hominy, rinsed and drained
1 can diced tomatoes
3 Hatch Green Chile, roasted, seeded
  & skinned
32 oz. chicken stock
1 tablespoon chili powder
1/2 teaspoon dried oregano
2 tablespoon ground cumin

1 teaspoon salt or to taste
1 teaspoon black pepper or to taste
1/2 cup chopped fresh cilantro
Lime wedges for garnish
Flour & Corn tortillas, warmed

Toppings
Shredded lettuce
Grated cheddar cheese
Chopped green onions
Diced avocado

Preheat oven to 350 degrees. In a Dutch oven over medium-high heat, warm oil. Add onion, bell pepper, garlic, and pork and saute until vegetables are tender and pork is browned. Stir in hominy, green chile, diced tomatoes, stock, seasonings.

Bake uncovered, until meat is tender and flavors are blended, about 40 minutes. Add cilantro, garnish with lime and serve with tortillas. Set out toppings in small bowls to add as desired.

Green Chile Enchilada Soup

Aaron Bensonhaver (Florida)

6-8 oz chopped roasted Green Chile (any variety, any heat)
1 26 oz can condensed cream of chicken soup
16 oz (1 lb) grilled or boiled chicken breast, chopped
1 tbsp hot red chile powder
2 tbsp ground cumin
2 tbsp granulated garlic
1 medium onion

2 tbsp extra virgin olive oil
12-15 corn tortillas
2 cups crushed corn tortilla chips
26 oz milk
1 tbsp black pepper
1 small/medium red or orange bell pepper, chopped
1/4 cup shredded cheese/serving after cooked.

Sweat/saute onion and bell pepper in a frying pan. Set aside.

Grill/boil chicken breast until cooked, chop into small pieces, set aside.

Mix soup mix and milk in a large mixing bowl. Soup will probably remain chunky, this is OK.

Add chile and all remaining spices to soup mix, stir.

Tear tortillas into small pieces, about 1-2 square inches each, mix into soup.

Add crushed tortilla chips to soup mix. Stir until all tortilla and chip pieces are at least coated in soup mixture.

Add chicken, onion and bell peppers.

Pour into a non-stick soup or stock pot, and heat on medium low heat (4 on an electric range), stirring every couple minutes to prevent sticking/burning.

Heat until condensed soup is thoroughly blended and all tortilla pieces are extremely soft.

Serve in soup bowls with shredded cheese.

Optional: use fajita sized flour tortillas to scoop out the soup, as opposed to a spoon.

Green Chili Gumbo

Bryan Benham (Colorado)

1 tbs veg. oil
1 med onion - chopped
4 oz all purpose flour or gluten free
    flour
4 oz butter
2 box Chicken Stock
1 rotisserie chicken - shredded
1 lb. Hatch green chili - diced - Hold
    back 1/2 cup for puree
1 tbs smoked paprika
1 tbs cumin
1 tsp salt or to taste
1 can black beans - drained and rinsed

1 1/2 cups frozen corn kernels
1 cup Mexican Crema
2 roasted pablano chilies
2 1/2 cups chopped cilantro
2 cups prepared rice
Juice of 1 lime
1 diced avocado
1/2 lb. crumbled queso fresco cheese
1 tbsp filé powder
Salt to taste

Heat pot and oil and sauté onion until translucent. Place stick of butter and slowly pour in flour to make the roux (you can remove the onion or leave it...it doesn't matter). When the roux gets to a light brown color add the 2 boxes of chicken stock bring to a boil. Add the chicken, green chili, paprika, cumin and salt. Simmer or put in a slow cooker and cook for 4 hours.

Add the corn and beans. Cook for another hour.

Lime Cilantro Rice

Make 2 cups of white or brown rice or get some Chinese take out. Add the lime and 1/2 cup of the chopped cilantro.

Poblano Cream

Add the Mexican creme to a blender (the magic bullet works great for this) add the 1/2 cup hatch green chile and the 2 roasted pablano and a tsp of salt. Blend until smooth.

Stir 1 cup of cilantro into the gumbo and cook for 15 additional minutes.

Serve over the rice and garnish with avocado, cheese, cilantro and filé powder.

Nothing but Green Green Chile! (Top 10 Grand Prize Winner)

Ian J. B. Kelley (Colorado)

For the chile base:
4 oz vegetable oil
16 full stalks of green onion, diced
4 tbsp. minced garlic
2 tbsp kosher salt
2 tbsp ground cumin
2 tbsp ground thyme
2 tbsp white pepper
4 tbsp lime juice
4 oz white vinegar (you may need to add 2-4 oz more depending on heat preferred.)
2 c. Mtn Dew (shhhhhh... don't tell...)
1 fresh dark green jalapeño (optional)

For the shredded pork:

1 shoulder of pork, bone in.
2 tbsp paprika
2 tbsp salt
2 tbsp black pepper
2 tbsp ground garlic
2 tbsp onion powder
6 bay leaves

For the soup base:
1 lb. Unsalted butter
1 lb. White enriched flour
1 bunch of fresh cilantro, chopped
8 oz. Minor's vegetable stock
1 gal. Filtered water
1 qt. Fresh water separate.

Begin by rubbing the pork in the seasonings mentioned above. Place in a half-pan and adding the bay leaves and enough water to nearly submerge.

Cover tightly in foil and slow-roast at 200° for 8 hours or until the meat is easily shredded and pulled from the bone. Drain and shred.

Place the diced green onion, minced garlic, oil and salt in a large stock pot. Saute until the garlic begins to brown. Add the optional jalapeño then.

Add 2 lbs. Hot diced chilies and saute for 5 minutes on medium high heat, allowing fond to form and scraping it away from the bottom of the pan repeatedly. Add the vinegar and lime juice and all seasonings

Add the shredded pork shoulder and mix thoroughly with a long male spoon. (Anything with slots or holes will collect the pork and be troublesome.) Add 1 qt of water and set aside.

In a 4 qt. saucepan, melt the butter. Sift and whisk the flour into the butter until the roux is combined thoroughly but remains somewhat loose, creamy and smooth.

In a separate pot, dissolve the vegetable stock in the gallon of water. Place the minced cilantro in the stock and bring to a boil. When the stock is at a rolling boil, shut off and begin whisking in the roux until it forms a vegetable gravy. (Fantastic on its own over turkey and mashed potatoes.)

Reheat the pork and chile mixture to a simmer and add the gravy, stirring constantly to avoid lumps. When the green chile is complete, add the mountain dew as the final touch. Stir until the reaction completes itself.

Let cool for 1 day for optimal flavor. Reheat and serve with a garnish of shredded cheddar and diced green onions alongside a freshly warmed flour tortilla!

To bring the heat and melt faces, add 1 finely diced jalapeño alongside the chiles.

Personal Notes: This recipe is the culmination of a lifetime of eating dozens of different recipes for green chile and took a year to complete.

Salads

CONVERSION OF PAN AND UTENSIL SIZES

UTENSIL	Measure (Volume)	Measure (cm)	Measure (inches)
Baking or cake pan	2 L	20 cm square	8-inch square
	2.5 L	23 cm square	9-inch square
	3 L	30x20x5	12x8x2
	3.5 L	33x21x5	13x9x2
Cookie sheet		40x30	16x12
Jelly roll pan	2 L	40x25x2	15x10x3/4
Loaf pan			
Round layer cake pan	1.2 L	20x4	8x1-1/2
			9x1-1/2
Pie pan	750 mL	20x3	8x1-1/4
	1 L	23x3	9x1-1/4
Tube pan	2 L	20x7	8x3
	3 L	23x10	9x4
Springform pan	2.5 L	23x6	9x3
	3 L	25x8	10x4
Baking dish	1 L		1 qt.
	1.5 L		1-1/2 qt.
	2 L		2 qt.
	2.5 L		2-1/2 qt.
	3 L		3 qt.
	4 L		4 qt.
Custard cup	200 mL		6 fl. oz.
Muffin pans	40 mL	4x2.5	1.5x1
	75 mL	5x3.5	2x1-1/4
	100 mL	7.5x3.5	3x1-1/2
Mixing bowls	1 L		1 qt.
	2 L		2 qt.
	3 L		3 qt.

Sauteed Chile Salad

Tishia Stewart (New Mexico)

1 Hatch green chile; sliced into thin
1/2 inch long pieces
1 each: red, yellow, and orange bell
pepper; thinly sliced into 1 inch
pieces
1 small onion (any); sliced into thin
one inch long pieces
1 tablespoon of Pampered Chef
Chili-Lime Rub

2 tablespoons of olive oil
2 tablespoons of Raspberry-Vinaigrette
Cold, Fresh organic spinach
Cold, Fresh red-leaf lettuce

Heat pan on med. heat with 2 tablespoons of olive oil.
Toss in green chilies, bell peppers, and onion.
Sprinkle chili-lime rub onto veggies, saute until hot, about 3
minutes.
Remove from heat.
Top salad greens with sauteed chilies, bell peppers, and onion. Add
Raspberry-vinaigrette.

Enjoy.

Chayote, Chile, and Cheese Salad

Laurie Smith (New Mexico)

2 chayotes
1 roasted green chile
1 roasted red bell pepper
3 ounces cheddar cheese
1 ripe, firm avocado

1/3 cup white wine vinegar
2 tablespoons extra virgin olive oil
2 tablespoons chopped fresh cilantro
1/2 cup thinly sliced green onions
salt and pepper

In a 3 to 4 quart pan, bring about 1-1/2 quarts of water to a boil.
Peel chayotes and cut into 1/2-inch cubes (soft seed is edible). Add
chayotes to water, and simmer until tender when pierced, about 10
minutes.

Drain, then plunge into ice water to stop cooking; drain again.
Stem and seed roasted chile and bell pepper and cut them into

1/4-inch squares. Dice cheese into 1/2 inch cubes. Peel and pit avocado and cut into 1/2-inch cubes. Combine ingredients in a large bowl.

Mix vinegar, oil, and cilantro, then add vinegar mixture, chayotes, and onions to vegetables in large bowl. Mix gently and season to taste.

Potato Salad New Mexico Style

Joyce Sizemore (Georgia)

5 lbs potatoes (red or Yukon gold)
1 medium sweet onion chopped fine
1- 4 oz can chopped green chilies or 1
   large roasted fresh green chile (more
   or less to taste)
1- 2 oz jar diced pimientos
4 eggs hard boiled and coarsely
   chopped
1 cup mayonnaise

1/2 cup salsa
1 tbsp fresh lime juice
1 tsp salt
1/2 tsp ground black pepper
Chopped fresh cilantro or parsley if
   desired.

Boil potatoes until fork tender, remove from water, and let cool until can hold to peel. Cut potatoes into bite size chunks.
In a large bowl, combine the potatoes, eggs, onion, pimientos and chile peppers.
Combine the mayonnaise, lime juice with salsa, and seasonings. Add to the potato salad and mix until well blended. If desired, add more mayonnaise.
If desired, garnish with chopped cilantro before serving.
Serves 8-10

Personal Notes: Warm potatoes gain and hold flavors better than letting them cool completely prior to mixing with other ingredients.

Quick Breads

EQUIVALENTS AND SUBSTITUTIONS

1 pound shelled walnuts	=	3 cups chopped walnuts
1 pound raisins	=	2-3/4 cups seedless raisins
1 pound dates	=	2-1/2 cups pitted dates
1 tablespoon cornstarch	=	2 tablespoons flour or 4 teaspoons tapioca
1 medium clove of garlic	=	1/8 tsp. garlic powder
1 cup honey	=	1 cup molasses or corn syrup
1 cup ketchup	=	1 cup tomato sauce plus 1/2 cup sugar plus 2 tablespoons vinegar
1 teaspoon dry mustard	=	1 tablespoon prepared mustard
1 small onion	=	1 tablespoon dried onion
1 cup tomato juice	=	1/2 cup tomato sauce plus 1/2 cup water
1 cup self-rising flour	=	1 cup flour plus 1-1/2 tablespoons baking powder plus 1/2 teaspoon salt
1 egg	=	1 teaspoon cornstarch
1 cup liquid honey	=	1-1/4 cups sugar plus 1/4 cup liquid
1 cup corn syrup	=	1 cup sugar plus 1/4 cup liquid
1 cup buttermilk	=	1 cup plain yogurt
1 cup sour cream	=	1 cup plain yogurt
1 cup tomato juice	=	1/2 cup tomato paste plus 1/2 cup water

Aunt Connie's Green Chile Cornbread

Martha Grose (Missouri)

2 Boxes Jiffy Corn Bread Mix
1 Box Yellow Cake Mix

1 Can Creamed Corn
1/2 - 1 Cup Chopped Fresh Roasted
Hatch Green Chilies

Prepare yellow cake batter according to box instructions.
Mix Jiffy Corn Bread mix with 1/2 cake batter, 1/2 can creamed corn and green chiles. Spread into greased 9x13 pan. Bake according to cake mix box.
Savor!!!

John's Mexican Cornbread

John Humphreys (Idaho)

1-1/4 cup all purpose flour
3/4 cup of corn meal
1/4 cup of sugar
2 tsp of baking powder
1/2 tsp of Salt - Optional
1 cup skim milk

1/4 cup vegetable oil
2 eggs
8 oz mixed slices of pepper jack and
cheddar cheese
8 oz can of Hatch Green Chile - I use hot,
use med or mild.
15 oz can of sweet corn/ Mexi-corn -
drained.

Preheat oven to 400 degrees
Spray an 8 in pan with Pam.

Take 2 mixing bowls: 1 for mixing all dry ingredients and 1 for mixing wet ingredients. After mixing add wet to dry. Add one third of chile and drained corn into the corn bread mix.

Pour a bottom layer of batter and cook for 7 minutes. Remove from oven, put a layer of sliced cheese and one third of chile on top. Then pour rest of batter on top and cook for 7 more minutes. Remove from oven again and put small squares of cheese and final one third of chile on top and return to oven for final 7 - 15 minutes baking, use a toothpick to check if cornbread is baked. When done, cut while still hot into squares and allow to cool on a plate.

Green Chile Corn Bread

Carter White (California)

2 medium-sized green chilies
1 cup (1 stick) butter
1 cup white sugar
4 eggs
1 (15 ounce) can cream-style corn
1/2 cup shredded Monterey Jack
  cheese

1/2 cup shredded Cheddar cheese
1 cup all-purpose flour
1 cup yellow cornmeal
4 teaspoons baking powder
1/4 teaspoon salt

Roast chilies (either on open flame grill or in cast-iron skillet) until skin is blackened. Let chilies cool in a paper bag, then peel chilies, removing stems and seeds, and chop to a medium dice.

Preheat oven to 300 degrees F. After oven is hot, preheat 12-inch cast-iron skillet with one tbsp of the butter.

Melt remainder of the butter in a microwave oven and blend it with the sugar in a large bowl. Beat in eggs one at a time. Blend in cream corn, chilies, and cheese.

In a separate bowl, stir together flour, cornmeal, baking powder and salt.

Add flour mixture to corn and chile mixture; stir until just mixed. Pour batter into prepared skillet.

Bake in preheated oven for 1 hour, until a toothpick inserted into center of the pan comes out clean.

Entrees & Sides

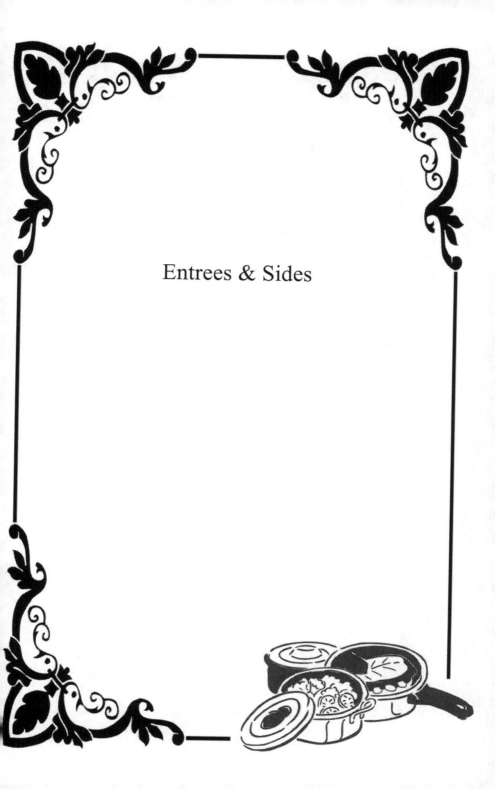

OVEN TEMPERATURE CHART

MISCELLANEOUS	Temp.	Minutes
Custard Cup	300F	20-30
Custard Casserole	300F	45-60
Soufflé	325F	50-60
Timbales	300F	35-45
Rice Pudding	325F	50-60

TABLE FOR DRIED FRUITS

FRUIT	Amount of Sugar or Honey	Cooking Time
Apricots	1/4 c. for each c. fruit	40 min.
Figs	1 tbsp. for each c. fruit	30 min.
Peaches	1/4 c. for each c. fruit	45 min.
Prunes	2 tbsp. for each c. fruit	45 min.

RULES FOR WHIPPING CREAM

- Chill the cream, bowl and beaters in a refrigerator for at least 2 hours. Beat until it is fairly stiff.
- If cream is beaten until it is warmer than 45 degrees, it will turn to butter.
- Should cream start to turn buttery, whip in 2 or 3 more tbsp. of cold milk.
- If you wish the cream to keep stiff for a day or two, add one teaspoon gelatine soaked in one tablespoon cold water. Dissolve the gelatine over hot water; allow to cool to the consistency of egg white before adding to the cream and whipping.
- Use medium speed when whipping cream with an electric beater.
- Cream, when whipped, almost doubles in bulk.

SUBSTITUTES FOR WHIPPING CREAM

1. Use light cream or cereal cream after allowing it to stand undisturbed for 48 hours in the refrigerator. Whip as you would whipping cream.
2. Prepare cream as given above. Soak 1 tsp. gelatine in 2 tbsp. cold water and dissolve over hot water. Allow to cool; then add to the cream and whip.
3. Use evaporated milk. Milk prepared with gelatine holds up better and longer, but may be more convenient to chill it on occasion. Chill 12 hours. Use medium speed on the electric beater when whipping.

Green Chile Grits With Shrimp

Don Shows (New Mexico)

6 cups BOILING WATER
1 1/2 cups grits
2 tsp salt
dash black pepper
1 1/2 sticks butter (melted)

1 lb sharp cheddar cheese, grated
½ pound raw shrimp, peeled & deveined
3 well beaten eggs
8-10 green chilies, peeled and chopped

Boil water, grits, and salt until thickened. Combine remaining ingredients and add to grits. Pour into greased baking dish and bake (uncovered) in 300° oven for about one hour.

Green Chili Meatloaf

Debbie Smith (Texas)

1 1/2 pound ground beef
1 whole finely chopped onion
1 cup finely chopped hatch green
  chilies
2 eggs
1/2 cup Italian bread crumbs

2 tablespoons honey
1 can Rotel with green chile
1 finely chopped bell pepper
1- 8 oz can of tomato sauce

Preheat oven to 400 degrees. Mix together in a large bowl all ingredients until well mixed. Place mixed ingredients into a glass baking dish (9 x13) and bake for 45 minutes. Top with ketchup to taste (optional) and bake for 15 more minutes. Serve hot! Makes about 10 servings.

Grilled Green Chile Wrapped Salmon

Wendi McClaren-Geis (Colorado)

6 oz salmon filets
Roasted whole green chile
Chopped garlic
Butter

Lemon
Salt
Pepper

Take salmon filet and place garlic, butter, lemon, salt, and pepper on it to taste. Filet and clean the roasted green chile. Wrap it entirely around all of the salmon. Wrap this in aluminum foil. Grill it on the BBQ for 15-20 min. This can be made in the oven as well. Cook at 350 degrees for 20-25 min.

Green Chile and Jalepeno Cornbread Pudding

Patrick Driscoll (Arizona)

3 green chilies – roasted, peeled, seeded and diced
1 or 2 fresh jalapeños – diced
2 eggs beaten
1 16 oz frozen white corn

1 16 oz can cream corn
1 8.5 oz box Jiffy Corn Bread mix
1 cup melted salted butter
1 and 1/4 cup sour cream

Pre-heat oven to 350 degrees F.
Mix all ingredients in a large bowl. Eggs last. Let stand for 10 minutes.
Pour into a 9" X 9" non-greased – (preferably Corning Ware) – baking dish.
Bake for 50 to 65 minutes.
Check with tooth pick in the middle – if it has no liquid on it when pulled – it's ready.
Serve with honey.

Green Chile Shepherd's Pie

Laura Hall (Washington)

1 pound ground beef
1 pound shredded sharp cheddar cheese
1 can of corn

3-4 cups of mashed potatoes
Lots of chopped green chile

Brown up your hamburger meat and drain all the grease. Put it in a casserole dish. Put a layer of cheese on the meat. In the same pan put the can of corn and the chopped green chile and warm up. Once warm, put the corn and chile mixture on the meat and cheese.

Add another layer of cheese. Then add the mashed potatoes and another layer of cheese. Put in the oven at 350° until all the cheese is melted.

Green Chile Fettuccine Alfredo

Rachel Johnson (New Mexico)

1/4 cup butter
1 cup heavy cream
1 clove garlic, crushed
1 1/2 cups freshly grated Parmesan
  cheese

1/4 cup chopped fresh parsley
4 large peeled, roasted, chopped green
  chilies
2 grilled chicken breasts (optional)

Melt butter in a medium saucepan over medium low heat. Add cream and simmer for 5 minutes, then add garlic and Parmesan cheese and whisk quickly, heating through. Stir in parsley, green chile and serve over warm fettuccine noodles. If you are using the chicken breasts, cut into long strips and lay on top, sprinkled with a little extra Parmesan.

Lamb Chops with Sweet Green Chili Sauce

Laurel Marshall (Nevada)

4 1" thick lamb shoulder or rib chops,
  American Lamb is best
1 Tbsp olive oil
6 cloves garlic peeled and crushed
Salt and pepper

1 cup chicken broth
1 cup apple jelly
1 1/2 cup chopped green chile (hotness to
  taste)

Heat olive oil in dutch oven to medium heat; salt and pepper lamb to taste; put garlic and lamb in pan cook till desired doneness approx 6-8 minutes per side turning once. Remove lamb to heated platter. In same pan add broth, stirring till boiling, scraping browned bits from bottom of pan, add jelly and chile, bring back to boil cook and stir for 2 minutes till jelly is melted and sauce thickens a little. Pour sauce over chops and serve immediately.

Serves 4

New Mexican Meat Loaf

Eddie Dehart (New Mexico)

2 pounds of ground chuck
1 chopped onion
5 chopped jalapeños
1/2 cup of chopped green chile
2 sticks of chopped celery
2 eggs
1 cup of bread crumbs or cracker crumbs
2 teaspoons of dry mustard

3 teaspoons of brown sugar
2 teaspoons of garlic powder
1 tablespoon of salt
1/2 tablespoon of black pepper
1/4 cup of Worcestershire sauce
Topping for meat loaf, 1/2 cup of ketchup 1/2 cup of hot sauce (mix all together)

In a large mixing bowl add all ingredients together and mix together till well blended. Shape into 2 (7-1/2 x 4-inch) loaves. Place in a sheet pan and roast at 350° for 40 to 50 minutes. Top with ketchup, hot sauce mix and heat in the oven till thick and server. Yields 5 servings.

Vigil Great Green Chili

Frances Vigil (New Mexico)

Frozen New Mexico roasted green chile 1 Bag- chopped
1 pound sirloin steak
1 medium white onion
2-3 cloves fresh garlic chopped

chicken stock
bacon grease 2-3 tablespoons
1 medium tomato diced
2 corn on the cob taking corn off the cob
salt to taste

Brown the sirloin steak, onion, and corn in the oil in a pan on medium heat until the steak is brown and the corn is slightly tender, once cooked drain the grease return to stove add the garlic and tomato stirring so nothing sticks to the pan. Add the chopped green chile add enough chicken stock to the pan about 3 cups adding more as needed. Let simmer 30 to 40 minutes, adding salt every time you add ingredients, salt to your taste. Enjoy!

Grandma Ollie's Chile Relleno Casserole

Debbie Ferreira (New Mexico)

16 whole green chilies
1 lb. sharp cheddar cheese- shredded
1 lb. jack cheese - shredded
1/4 cup flour

1/2 tsp. salt
1 can evaporated milk
4 eggs
2 8 oz. cans tomato sauce

Line baking dish (large baking dish-14" X 11") with 8 green chilies. Top with cheddar cheese. Line next layer with 8 remaining chilies. Top with jack cheese. Beat flour, salt, and small amount of milk to make paste. Beat in rest of milk and eggs and pour over chilies and cheese. Bake in preheated 325 degree oven for 1 hour. Remove from oven and pour tomato sauce over top.
Return to oven and bake 20-30 more minutes until set.
Remove from oven, let cool 10 minutes before serving.
Enjoy!

Taos Shepherd's Pie

Amanda Green (Alabama)

1-2 lbs. ground beef, locally raised if
 possible
1 packet dry onion soup mix
6 russet potatoes, cubed, cooked, and
 mashed

1- 6 oz can fire roasted Hatch green
 chilies, not drained
1-1/2 cups cheese
Small bag of frozen English peas and
 carrots, thawed

Preheat oven to 350 degrees

Cook, brown, and drain ground beef. Then add the dry onion soup mix with the canned green chilies. Let stand until mixture looks coated onto beef. You might have to add a little water if the canned chilies do not provide enough moisture. Do not add enough water to make soupy.

Next, get a 9 x 13 inch casserole dish and coat well with cooking spray.

Pour the cooked beef and chilies mixture onto bottom of pan. Then layer thawed frozen peas and carrots. Next, layer mashed potatoes. Finally, top with 1-1/2 cups of Cheddar cheese.

Put into preheated oven until cheese is bubbly, about 15 minutes.

Green Chili Rice

Henry Lombrana (Texas)

1 Cup of Extra Long Grain Enriched Rice
Olive Oil
1 Medium Size Bell Pepper (Chop & Dice)
¼ Medium Size Yellow Onion (Chop & Dice)
1 Stalk of Celery (Chop & Dice)
2 Cloves of Garlic (Use Garlic Press)

2 Medium Size & Mild Hatch Peppers (Chop & Dice)
1 Medium Size Tomato (Chop & Dice)
2 Cups of Chicken Broth
1 Teaspoon of Cumin
2 Teaspoons of Powdered Chicken & Tomato Bouillon
2 Stems of Cilantro (Chop)

On medium heat brown your rice with enough olive oil. Just before the rice is completely brown, add the bell peppers, yellow onions, celery, and crushed garlic. Stir in and for a few minutes. Add the Hatch peppers and tomatoes and stir for another minute or two. Add the chicken broth, 1 teaspoon of cumin, and powdered bouillon and bring to boil. Once the rice starts to boil, stir in the cilantro, cover and simmer until the rice is ready. (Approximately 8 minutes)

Cowboy Quiche

Betty Brooks (New Mexico)

12-18 roasted/peeled/split green chilies
1 lb. Colby Jack cheese, grated
1/2 c. finely diced onion

1 1/2 c. milk
4 large eggs
1/2 to 3/4 package saltines, very finely crumbled

Set oven at 375 degrees and use a 9x13" pan.

Spray pan with Pam.
Place a single layer of green chile on bottom of pan.
Sprinkle grated cheese evenly over chile.
Sprinkle diced onion over cheese.
Place second layer of green chile over cheese/onion.
Blend milk and eggs and pour over chile/cheese.
Finely crumble saltines and sprinkle evenly over casserole.
Pat flat with hand on surface onto milk/egg.
Cover with Saran wrap and let sit in refrigerator for at least one hour so crackers can soak up milk mixture.
Bake 30-45 minutes or until browned and puffy.
Crackers form a soft crust on the top.
Serve with pinto beans and cabbage slaw.

Rio Grande Souffle

Robert Pirtle (New Mexico)

12 oz. roasted green chile chopped (Heritage Big Jim)
2 cups shredded monterey-jack cheese
1 small purple onion
5 large eggs
1/2 tsp cumin
1 tsp salt

1 tsp garlic powder
10" quiche pan

Optional Ingredients:
12 oz can diced tomatoes
bacon crumbs, or any meat diced (ie. ground taco meat, leftover steak or grilled pork)

Preheat oven to 450
Spray pan with nonstick spray oil. (I use butter flavored) Dice onion and mix with chile, cheese and any meat used.
Spread in pan and sprinkle with salt.
Separate egg whites from yolks. Beat whites until stiff and forming peaks.
Mix cumin and garlic powder in yolks and fold into whites.
Pour over chile-cheese mixture and bake.
Check souffle at 30 minutes, sides should be pulling away and withstand a tooth pick test, at this time you may top with diced tomatoes or cheese and bake for another 15 minutes.
serves 4 to 6 people.

Quick Spanish Rice

Arnold Montoya (New Mexico)

2 tbsp oil
10 slices pre-cooked bacon
1 cup diced onion
1/2 cup diced red and green bell
  peppers
1 tsp salt
1 tsp pepper

1 tsp garlic
1 cup Minute Rice
1 - 14.5 oz can stewed tomatoes (sliced
  Roma style tomatoes w/oregano &
  basil)
2 tbsp tomato paste
2 cups water
1 cup finely diced roasted green chile
  peppers

Saute in 2 tbsp oil
10 slices pre-cooked bacon
1 cup diced onion
½ cup diced red and green bell peppers
1 tsp salt
1 tsp pepper
1 tsp garlic
1 cup minute rice

Then add
1 - 14.5 oz can stewed tomatoes (sliced Roma style tomatoes
w/oregano & basil)
2 tbsp tomato paste
2 cups water

Simmer about 20 minutes until most of the liquid has evaporated.

Add 1 cup of finely diced roasted green chile peppers simmer just long enough to heat the green chili and serve. Do not cook roasted green chile, simply re-heat when adding to the rice.

Apricot Chile Marmalade

Beth Stephens (New Mexico)

Fresh Apricots
Roasted Green Chile
Several fresh lemons
Sugar

Sea Salt (red or brown preferable)
Pectin
8 oz. Mason Jars
Deep pressure cooker or tall pot to boil
jars

Boil fresh apricots keeping in mind that each 4 jar batch of marmalade will hold the equivalent of 3 cups of cooked fruit, 3 cups of sugar and 1/2 cup of pectin.
Ideally you will prepare jars in batches no larger than this at a time for consistency.

Boil the Apricots for 20-30 minutes. Cool, then peel and pit. (Boil all the Apricots you can get a hold of).

For each 3 cups of mashed apricot add 5-6 chopped chiles (peeled and unseeded), 3 cups of sugar, about a teaspoon of sea salt and 1/2 cup pectin.
Boil the mixture briefly and sir it up well.

Prepare your jars according to canning directions of your choice. Cool slowly then store in cool place until gifted to grateful friends and neighbors!

Green Chile Chicken Chilaquiles

Randall Stwalley (Colorado)

1 lb Hatch green chile
1 lb thinly sliced boneless skinless
  chicken breast
1/4 cup minced yellow onion
3 cloves garlic minced
24 yellow corn tortillas

2 cups cooking oil
1 tsp salt
1 tsp black pepper
1 1/2 cups Monterey Jack cheese,
  shredded
2 tbsp coarse sea salt

Add salt, pepper, garlic, onion, green chile and chicken to crock pot, slow cooking for 6-8 hours.

Once cooked, use forks to shred chicken in crock pot and let stand for half hour to marry and infuse flavors.

In a large skillet, pour in 2 cups of cooking oil and set heat to just over medium.

Cut tortillas into 1 1/2" slices (should get 4 portions per tortilla). Fry strips in oil until golden brown and crispy. Drain onto paper towel to remove excess oil and sprinkle each batch with a little sea salt. Repeat until finished.

Lay fried tortilla strips on baking sheet and layer with shredded chicken and chile mixture. Sprinkle with cheese and place into preheated oven for 15 minutes on 350 degrees.

Hatch Green Chili Souffle

Rebecca Allen (California)

5 egg whites
4 egg yolks
3 Tbps butter
3 Tbsp flour
1 cup warmed nonfat milk

1 cup peeled diced Hatch green chilies
1/4 cup shredded Swiss cheese
Butter and grated Parmesan to line the
  souffle dish
1/2 tsp cream of tartar
1/2 tsp. nutmeg

Coat dish with butter and dust with Parmesan.
Heat oven to 400 degrees.
Warm milk. Do not boil.

Heat butter and make a roux with the flour. Cook until flour begins to color. Stir in milk. Whisk until it thickens. Whisk in 4 egg yolks. Add Swiss cheese, chilies and nutmeg. Set aside.

Beat egg whites and the cream of tartar until soft peaks form.

Stir a quarter of the egg whites into the chili- cheese mixture. Fold the rest of the egg whites into the mixture.

Gently pour into prepared souffle dish.

Bake in 400-degree oven for 5 minutes. Lower heat to 375 and bake for 35 minutes. Don't open the oven to peek!!

Divide into 2-4 portions and serve with a tossed green salad.

Chili Rellenos

Lorale McConley (Colorado)

12 Whole, roasted green chilies
Monterey Jack Cheese (cut in 1/4"
  strips about 3" long) Sliced Ham
  (Very thinly sliced, not quite shaved)
2 beaten eggs (several tbsp water)
1 cup flour in flat plate
1 cup cracker meal in flat plate
1 1/2 cups Vegetable Oil

Sauce for Top of Chilies:
1 Large Onion (diced)
2 cloves garlic (pressed)
2 TBLS Vegetable Oil
16 oz Tomato Sauce

Dry the green chilies on paper towels. Wrap a piece of cheese with a slice of ham. Insert the ham/cheese into chili. Dip into egg, cover entire chili, then roll in the flour, then back into the egg, then roll in the cracker meal. Place gently into HOT 1/2 vegetable oil in a large skillet.
Do the same for the rest of the chilies. When golden brown and the melted cheese starts to ooze from the chile remove and drain on paper towels.

Sauce for over top of Chilies

Put the oil in a hot skillet, add onion and cook a couple of minutes add garlic and get ready for an awesome aroma. When the onions are clear add the tomato sauce and lower heat and cook down to a gravy consistency.

Calabacita Casserole

Kathy Mondragon (New Mexico)

1 ½ lb of ground turkey

1 onion (medium or large size) chopped

6-9 medium size or small summer squash. (I usually mix 2 or 3 zucchini with 2 or 3 yellow or crookneck squash or 2 or 3 Mexican summer squash. Looks great with the different colors)

1 bag of frozen corn (I think the regular size bag is 16 oz)

½ lb medium hot chopped green chilies (more or less to taste)

1-2 cups yellow cheese (I always use Velveeta for cooking because it melts smooth and does not separate)

2-3 cloves of fresh garlic chopped (or you can use garlic powder approx 1 Tbsp)

Corn Tortilla chips.

Fry the turkey in a large skillet. Salt and pepper to taste. Add the onion and garlic to the meat and fry till onion is cooked.
Add the green chili.
Wash and slice the squash into approx 1-2 inch cubes and add to skillet.
Cover and cook till squash is tender. Add bag of corn and cheese. Stir till cheese is melted (you can add some milk or chicken broth to thin out the cheese if necessary). Serve with crushed tortilla chips on top.
Enjoy!

Green Chile Salmon Croquettes

Peggy A. Nelson (New Mexico)

1 can (14.5 ounce salmon (drained and chopped) bones & skin removed
1/4 cup dried bread crumbs
5 saltine crackers
small onion chopped-- about 1/4 cup worth
2 roasted and peeled chopped green chilies. (remove tops and seeds)
2 eggs

1/8 teaspoon lemon juice

For Topping:
2 tablespoon of light mayonnaise and 1 teaspoon mustard (dijon-style or regular)
1 small green chile chopped

In a bowl combine salmon, bread crumbs, crumbled saltine crackers, onion, eggs, green chile, and lemon juice.
Mix well.
Shape into 4 - 6 patties about 1/2 inch thick.
Melt butter or olive oil in a large skillet.
Cook over a medium heat.
Add salmon- green chile croquettes to skillet. Cook until brown and flip and brown on other side.
You can also bake these in a 425 degree oven for 15-20 minutes flipping over after about 8 minutes. Be sure to spray coat the baking sheet and spray the tops of the croquettes.
When finished cooking. serve with topping of mayonnaise, mustard and chopped green chile or place topping in a small dish to the side.
Serves 4.

Green Chili & Cheese Fritatta (Top 10 Grand Prize Winner)

Barbara Rose Farber (New Mexico)

3 Tbsp. unsalted butter
1 white onion, finely diced
12 roasted green chilies, peeled, seeded & diced, (I use 1/2 mild & 1/2 medium, Biad Chili of course!)
8 extra large eggs, well beaten

1 Tbsp. ground cumin
Salt & Pepper to taste
3 cups shredded Jack & Cheddar cheese blend
Warmed flour tortillas
Homemade salsa

Preheat oven to 350 degrees.
Spray a large oven proof skillet with a no-stick spray.
Melt the butter till it begins to froth, do not let the butter burn.
Add the diced onion to the skillet, cook until the onion is translucent.
Add the green chili to the skillet, stir to blend them with the onion.
Add the ground cumin, salt & pepper to the beaten eggs, pour into the skillet.
Working from the edges of the skillet, lift the cooked egg and let the uncooked portions run underneath. continue until the top of the Fritatta is just a bit uncooked.
Add all the shredded cheese, and mix it gently into the remaining soft uncooked egg.
Bake at 350 degrees for 25 minutes, until the Fritatta has puffed up and the cheese is slightly browned.
Serve cut into wedges with warmed tortillas and salsa if desired.
Serves 4 to 6.

Chicos Pablito

Paul Kmetko (California)

6 ounces chicos (smoked dried corn)
2 cups dried pinto beans cleaned and
  rinsed
1 large yellow onion peeled and
  coarsely chopped
2 cloves garlic chopped
1 bay leaf

1/4 tsp. ground cumin
1/8 tsp cayenne pepper
3/4 cup New Mexico chile, seeded and
  chopped
3/4 lb smoked bacon lardons cut into 1/2
  inch cubes Salt (optional)

Soak the chicos and beans in an ample quantity of water for at least 4hrs, preferably overnight.
Saute the lardons in a stew pot until golden brown. Remove the lardons and discard all but 2 tablespoons of the pan drippings. Saute the onion and garlic in the pan drippings until the onion is transparent. Drain the chicos and beans. Put all of the ingredients together in the pot and then add just enough water to cover by 1/2 inch.
Bring to boil, cover pan and simmer over med low heat, until the beans and chicos are tender, (about 2 to 3 hours) adding water if necessary. The beans are done when they are soft and creamy but not mushy.The chicos will be soft but still chewy. Salt to taste.
Serve in bowls with a dollop of sour cream and cornbread and honey butter on the side.
Serves 6.
Source for chicos www.cibolojunction.com

Chile Relleno Meatballs (Top 10 Grand Prize Winner)

Maria Rocha (New Mexico)

2 c green chile
4 lbs ground hamburger meat
  uncooked
2 tsp each salt, pepper, garlic, cumin,
  oregano 2c grated of you favorite
  cheese
1-1/2 tbsp flour
3 eggs

2 c oil
2 large bowl for mixing
1 small bowl
Frying pan

First start out by mixing the hamburger meat, green chile, salt, pepper, garlic, cumin, oregano, and cheese together in the large bowl. After everything is mixed well put the bowl aside. Now get the small bowl and beat all 3 eggs together. Now that everything is mixed get the flour and the last large mixing bowl and put the flour in it. Make the meatballs. You can make your meatballs as big or small as you want. While you are making the meatballs put your oil on so it will be hot enough to start cooking. Once you have all the meatballs made, roll them in your egg first. Make sure they are completely coated with egg, then coat them in the flour, and put them in the frying pan. Cook the meatballs until golden brown, check the middle to make sure that they are done all the way through. Let cool for several minutes just so that you don't burn you mouth with the cheese. Enjoy your Chile Relleno Meatballs!

Vegetarian Enchilada Casserole

Jim Arnold (Texas)

8 corn Tortillas
One 15oz can of Hatch Crushed
 Tomatillos
One 4oz can of Hatch Fire Roasted
 Diced Green Chili
One 5oz size of Goat Milk Yogurt

Kraft or similar Mexican cheese blend
2 medium yellow squash
One medium sweet onion
One bunch fresh spinach

Preheat oven to 350.

Saute sliced yellow onion in extra virgin olive oil and add thinly sliced squash when onion is almost done.
Cook fresh spinach separately or along with the squash and onion.

Mix together 15 oz can of Hatch Crushed Tomatillos, 5 oz can mild or hot Hatch diced fire roasted chili, and the Goat Milk Yogurt and set in refrigerator until ready to use.

Spray glass casserole dish with non-stick product. Lay in overlapping 4 corn tortillas.

When vegetables are ready, start by adding the squash and onion mix on top of the first layer of tortillas.
Add 1/3 of the Tomatillo mix.
Add a layer of Mexican cheese (more or less depending on how much you want).
Add a layer of drained spinach on top of cheese.
Add another 1/3 of the tomatillo mixture.
Add the top layer of 4 overlapping corn tortillas.
Pour on the remaining 1/3 of the mixture and then top with a thin layer of Mexican blend cheese.

Bake uncovered in oven for 20-30 min.

Serve as a side dish or entre.

The Best Thanksgiving Dressing EVER!
Kim Smith Casford (New Mexico)

5 Cups Corn Bread, cooled completely
1 1/2 Cups Seasoned Bread Crumbs
1 Onion Finely Chopped
6 celery stalks, Finely Chopped
1 can sliced water chestnuts, finely chopped
1 pound sage flavored sausage, cooled and cooled
1/2 pound bacon, finely chopped, cooked and cooled, reserve grease
1 cup cheddar jack cheese, finely grated

1 cup pinon nuts, slightly roasted
1-2 cups roasted, peeled green chile, finely chopped
1 stick melted butter
Chicken stock
Poultry seasoning
Garlic
Fresh ground Pepper

In a large pan, saute the onion and celery in bacon grease, until onions are opaque.

In large bowl, crumble corn bread, add bread crumbs. Add onions and celery to bread mixture. Mix thoroughly. Add water chestnuts, sausage, bacon, cheese, pinon and chile and mix again. Add butter and mix again. Add chicken stock as need to make mixture wet, but not soaked. Additional melted butter can be used as well. Add poultry season, garlic and pepper to taste.

Bake covered at 325 degrees for 30 minutes. Remove cover and bake an addition 10 minutes, or until top is golden brown.

Personal Notes: We love green chile, so I use 2 cups, but you can adjust the amount of chile to suit your family and friends tastes.

Tortilla Hash

Dana Wagenhoffer (New Mexico)

1 13x9 Pan
2 lb of lean hamburger
1 pkg of 1 dozen corn tortillas
1 lb of Hatch NM green chile chopped (roasted & peeled)
1 Med Onion chopped (diced)
1 Green Bell Pepper (diced)
2 6oz cans of tomato sauce

1 1 lb package of Montary Jack cheese
1 16 0z can of stewed tomatoes
3 cloves of garlic chopped fine
1 TBSP salt or to desired taste
1 16 oz can of yellow corn
2 inches cooking oil

Prepare package of spanish rice in 2 quart pan per instructions on packaging.
Cook 1 LB of hamburger in a frying pan, add onions, bell peppers, garlic & salt to the cooking. Drain grease from fry pan when hamburger is done cooking. Return to pan and add chopped green chile (Hatch variety), tomato sauce, tomatoes, & drained can of corn to mixture bring to a simmer on low.
Heat 2 in cooking oil in frying pan, when hot cook all 12 corn tortillas, place on paper towels to soak up grease.

In 13x9 pan layer 6 corn tortillas on bottom of pan (3 on each side)then put some of the hamburger mixture on the corn tortillas, you can add cheese also. Add the last six corn tortillas to the top & repeat with remainder of hamburger mixture. Cover top of layer completely with cheese. Bake in 375 degree oven for 20 minutes. Cut & serve.

This recipe can be changed up to suit any ones liking. Use hominy

instead of corn. Add a layer of Spanish rice.
Can be served with guacamole, sour cream, picante etc...

Green Chili and Sauteed Onion Goat Cheese Tart

Tamar Sisneros (Washington)

1 1/2 cups flour
13 tbsp. unsalted butter, divided
1/2 tsp. salt, divided
3 – 4 tbsp. ice water
1/2 cup onion, chopped
1/2 cup peeled, cleaned and chopped
  green chile

10 oz. goat cheese
1 cup heavy cream
3 large eggs
1/4 tsp. paprika
1/8 tsp. ground black pepper

Begin preparing crust by cutting 12 tbsp. butter into the flour and 1/4 tsp. salt. Add water and mix only until crumbly. Gather dough into a loose ball, wrap in plastic wrap and refrigerate for half an hour. Pre-heat oven to 350°F. After refrigeration, roll out dough into a circle large enough to fill a 9 inch tart or pie pan, and put in pan. Cut off excess dough. Butter a piece of aluminum foil and fit it into the pan butter side down. Fill foil with beans, or rice to weigh down the crust. Bake crust for 20 minutes, then remove foil and beans or rice. Poke the crust all over with a fork and bake for 10 more minutes or until golden brown.

While crust is baking sauté the onion and green chile in the remaining butter. Place goat cheese in food processor and process until crumbly. Add cream, eggs, the rest of the salt, pepper, and paprika and process until well mixed.

Spread sautéed onions and chile over bottom of tart crust then pour goat cheese and egg mixture into the crust. Bake for 30-40 minutes until tart is firm when shaken, and slightly browned.

Allow to cool for 10 minutes before serving to allow filling to set.

Baked Green Chile Rellenos

Russell Stone (Wisconsin)

- 4 large whole roasted green chilies
- 1/2 cup re-fried beans
- 1/4 cup shredded Monterrey Jack cheese
- 3 Tbsp cream cheese
- 1 cup cornmeal
- 1/2 cup flour
- 1 tsp baking powder
- 1 Tbsp maple syrup
- 1 cup milk
- 1 tsp vinegar
- 1 tsp salt
- pinch of green or red chile powder
- 1 tsp garlic powder
- 1/2 tsp pepper

Turn your oven on to broil and move the top rack up to 2 rungs below the top. Place green chilies on a sheet pan and broil until the skins turn black, carefully turning so that they are evenly charred. When they are charred put them in a bowl and cover with plastic wrap. Let sit for 5 minutes and turn the oven down to 375F. Meanwhile mix together the beans, cheese, and cream cheese in a bowl with a little salt and pepper. In another bowl mix together all of the remaining ingredients. After 5 minutes remove the green chilies from the bowl and carefully peel off the charred skins. Cut a slit in each green chile from the top to bottom and carefully remove the seeds. If you leave a few in and it is not a big deal, but if you absolutely want to remove them all then go for it. Stuff 1/4 of the bean mixture into each green chile and close the slit tightly. Dip each stuffed green chile into the cornmeal mixture and let the excess drip off.

Place on a baking sheet lined with parchment. Bake at 375F for about 10 minutes until the cornmeal mixture is baked. Serve hot with salsa, rice, and chips!

Green Chile Stew (Top 10 Grand Prize Winner)
Susan Hershberger (Arizona)

1 ½ lbs. pork sirloin roast
½ C. flour
¼ t. black pepper
½ t. coarse ground or kosher salt
2-4 T. canola oil
½ chopped onion
2 minced cloves of garlic
1 ½ t. cumin

1 can tomato sauce (8 oz. size)
12 cherry/small tomatoes or two large tomatoes chopped
1 C. chopped carrots
2 C. boiling water
1 T. Worcestershire Sauce
1 C. green chilies, roasted, peeled and chopped up (mild were used here)
1 can mushrooms (8 oz. size) fresh would be okay too, I just had canned on-hand
1 large potato chopped into chunks, washed with skin left on

Place the flour, salt, and black pepper in a plastic bag and toss the meat in the bag until coated with the flour. Place half of the canola oil in a Dutch oven and heat up the oil. Add one-half of the pork and cook on all sides until brown. Don't crowd the meat or you won't get a good browning. Then push the cooked pork pieces to the side, add the rest of the oil. Add the rest of the pork and cook on all sides until brown. Add the onions, garlic, cumin, tomato sauce, tomatoes, carrots, boiling water, and Worcestershire sauce. Stir until mixed.

Stir in the green chilies.

Bring to a nice boil and reduce the heat to simmering.

Simmer this for one hour, stirring frequently. Then add the mushrooms and potato.

Bring to a boil and then reduce to a simmer. Simmer for one more hour, stirring frequently. It is best cooled, refrigerated, and served the next day with warm tortillas!

Personal Notes: Left over Green Chile Stew is an exceptional topping for cheese enchiladas!

Creamy Green Chile Chicken Enchiladas

Marie Gherghei (Ohio)

1 rotisserie chicken (2 ½ cups shredded chicken)
12 corn tortillas
2 cups low sodium chicken broth
1 large Spanish onion - diced
3 fresh garlic pieces - diced
1 cup Hatch roasted green chilies - diced
2 tablespoons cilantro - chopped
1 tablespoon red chile powder

1 cup monterey jack cheese - shredded
2 cups white cheddar cheese - shredded
2 tablespoons butter
2 tablespoons flour
1 cup sour cream
Salt/pepper to taste
Cilantro/Lime for garnish

Preheat oven to 350.

Heat 1 tablespoon oil in skillet over med heat. Fry tortillas one at a time – just to soften.

Heat 1 tablespoon oil in skillet over med heat. Add onion and garlic – sauté for a few mins until onions are cooked. Add 1/2 of the green chilies. Sauté another minute. Remove from heat.

Mix shredded chicken, garlic/onion/chile mix, 2 tablespoons cilantro, zest of 1 lime, 1 tablespoon red chile powder, monterey jack cheese…season with salt/pepper. Add 1/4 to 1/2 cup chicken broth and mix well.

Heat 2 tablespoons of butter over medium heat. Add 2 tablespoons of flour…whisk for a few minutes. Add 1 1/2 cups chicken broth – whisk together and cook for a few mins until mixture thickens a bit. Add the other 1/2 cup green chilies. Add 1 cup sour cream and 1 1/2 cups white cheddar cheese. Season w/salt and pepper.

Ladle a few spoonfuls of white chile sauce into a 9x13 pan. Spoon chicken mixture into tortillas – roll up and place in pan (tortillas should be touching). Pour the rest of the chile sauce over tortillas. Top with the rest of the 1/2 cup of cheese. Bake 25 mins – top with more cilantro and a fresh lime squeeze.

Green Chili Pot Pie

Sara Anderson (Colorado)

2 cups assorted veggies if fresh trim to bite size pieces and par cook to al dente if frozen, simply thaw a few minutes
4 cloves garlic minced
1/2 large onion diced
1 cup roasted peeled seeded chopped green chili - mild / medium are best for crowds
1 1/2 cup cooked chicken diced

6 tbsp butter divided

6 tablespoons flour
1 - 2 cups rich chicken stock

1 cup shredded cheese (American, Monterrey, or Havarti are all good choices)

Crust
1 sheet puffed pastry

Preheat oven to 375 degrees.

Saute garlic / onions in 2 tbsp butter till translucent. Add chilies and veggies to mixture, warm through. Add diced chicken to mixture and continue warming in a sauce pan.

Melt the remaining butter and then add the 6 tbsp flour. Whisk until smooth and creamy looking, then add 1 cup of the broth and continue whisking until smooth and velvety. Add the 1 cup of shredded cheese. Stir until cheese has melted and is creamy in consistency. Now add the veggie meat mixture from above to the sauce pan.

There should be enough liquid in this to make this all saucy like, this is where the remaining chicken stock comes in - add remaining broth until sauce fully envelopes the goodies in a rich creamy sauce.

Place this mixture in a well buttered 9x13 glass pan.

Then follow the directions on the package of the puffed pastry. Generally thaw for about 30 min prior to needing and then roll out on counter, prick with fork to avoid it over-rising then place over the mixture in the pan. Trim to fit and bake at 375 degrees for

20-30 minutes until golden and bubbly - yummalicious. Bake for 30 minutes or until top is golden brown and the mix is bubbly underneath.

Green Chili Frittata with Broccoli and Cheddar (Top 10 Grand Prize Winner)

Maria Ifill (New Mexico)

2/3 cup fresh bread crumbs
1/4 cup plus 1 tsp. extra-virgin olive oil
1/4 lb roasted diced green chile (seeded and peeled)
1/4 lb. broccoli, roughly chopped
1 1/2 roasted red peppers (pimiento), finely diced
12 eggs, lightly beaten
1 cup grated sharp cheddar cheese

3/4 tsp. kosher salt,
½ tsp freshly ground black pepper
1 fresh rosemary sprig
1 small onion, diced
1 garlic clove, minced
1/8 tsp. of quality red chili powder

Bring a small saucepan of water to a boil over high heat. Add the chopped broccoli and red pepper and cook until just tender, about 2 minutes. Drain and rinse with cold water. Transfer to a paper towel-lined plate. Add chopped green chile to broccoli/red pepper mixture.

In a large bowl, stir together the eggs, 1/2 cup of the cheese, the 3/4 tsp.
salt and black pepper, to taste. Set aside.

In the deep half of a frittata pan over medium heat, warm 2 Tbs. of the olive oil. Add the rosemary and onions and cook, stirring constantly, until the onions are translucent, about 3-5 minutes. Add the broccoli, spinach, red peppers, garlic and red chili powder, and season with salt and black pepper. Cook-- stirring occasionally-- for 2 minutes. Remove the rosemary and discard.

Reduce the heat to medium-low and pour in the egg mixture. Cook, using a rubber spatula to lift the cooked edges and allow the uncooked eggs to flow underneath, until the eggs are just beginning to set, about 8 minutes.

In the shallow pan over medium-low heat, warm the remaining 1 tsp. olive oil. Place the shallow pan upside down on top of the deep pan and flip the frittata into the shallow pan. Cook, covered, until the eggs are set, 7 to 8 minutes. Uncover the pan and sprinkle the frittata with the remaining 1/2 cup cheese and the bread crumbs. Transfer the pan to the oven and cook until the cheese is melted, about 1 minute.

Slide the frittata onto a plate and let rest for 5 minutes before serving.
Serves 8.

New Mexico Style Chile Verde

Ann Walsh (North Carolina)

1 2 lb. boneless pork loin roast	1 Tbs. olive oil
2 large yellow or white onions (or use 3 medium size)	1 lb roasted Hatch chiles, peeled and de-seeded
1 qt. chicken stock (if using canned, choose the low sodium variety)	1 28 oz. can tomatillos, rinsed and drained
1-1/2 tsp. garlic powder	1/4 tsp. PLUS 1 tsp. ground cumin
1/4 tsp sweet smoked paprika	1/4 c. Wondra (or equivalent thickener)
salt and pepper to taste	

1. Pre-heat oven to 350 degrees. Rub outside of pork with olive oil, then season with garlic powder, paprika, and ground black pepper. Do not to trim any fat on the loin roast. The meat will benefit from any added flavor and moisture from the rendered fat.
2. Place meat on roasting pan with 1/4-inch water. Cover tightly with foil, and roast undisturbed for 30 minutes. Uncover the meat and continue to roast for 20 minutes.
3. While meat is cooking, rough chop the onions and cut the Hatch Chilies length-wise first, and then slice horizontally into 1-inch sections. Set aside until meat is cooled.
4. When meat has finished roasting, allow it to cool long enough

so that it is able to be cut into 2-inch cubes by hand.

5.Place all meat,any residual pan juice, chicken stock, and onions into a

6-quart slow cooker. Cook on HIGH for 2 hours. Stir occasionally to help break the meat cubes into shreds.

6. Once the onions have softened, add the chiles and tomatillos. Continue to cook on HIGH for 2 hours. *(If you want to add more garlic powder, NOW is the time. Adding it earlier can make it bitter)

7. Add thickener half hour before serving time. Turn slow cooker down to LOW, stirring well to prevent lumps in the liquid. Allow the verde to cook down to desired thickness. Liquid in the chile verde should be loose consistency - like that of a cream soup.

8. Serve chile verde in bowls with warmed tortillas, and freshly chopped onions, grated cheese,and sour cream if desired for garnish. Buen provecho!

Tortilla Española with Fire-Roasted Green Chile (Top 10 Grand Prize Winner))

Marie Perucca-Ramirez (California)

2 tablespoons olive oil
½ pound white or red potatoes (do not use russets), sliced
1/16–inch thick
1 Spanish onion, about 6 ounces, sliced vertically in
1/16–inch pieces or diced

1½ teaspoons kosher salt (3/4 teaspoon table salt) ¼ teaspoon freshly ground black pepper
4 large eggs
6 fire-roasted New Mexico Green Chilies (use "Joe E. Parker"
chilies—or, for more kick, we use "Big Jims"), peeled,
seeded, stems removed, and chopped

Preheat the oven to 400 degrees.

Put the oil in a 10-inch Teflon sauté pan over medium heat and add the potatoes and onions and toss a few times to make sure the vegetables are coated with the oil; cook for 10 minutes stirring gently to brown the potatoes and onions evenly. While cooking, sprinkle the salt and pepper evenly over the mixture. When potatoes and onions are browned, add the chopped roasted green chilies and mix gently.

Beat the eggs with a tablespoon of water in a medium bowl using a wire whisk; add the eggs to the golden brown potatoes and onions. Using a rubber spatula, incorporate the egg mixture with the potato, onion and green chile mixture, being careful not to smash the potatoes. Cook for 3 minutes on top of the stove to set the bottom of the tortilla; then transfer the pan with the tortilla to the middle rack of the pre-heated oven. Cook for 5 minutes to finish cooking the eggs. Remove from oven carefully so as not to burn yourself; separate the tortilla from the pan by using a spatula (it should come out easily if it is cooked; if it's runny, return to the oven and finish cooking it for a minute or two more). Let it rest before serving.

Note: In Spain, the tortilla is usually cut into wedges and served at room temperate or cold.

Personal Notes: A tortilla is a "little cake" in Spain–not a taco wrapper. A cousin of the frittata, the Spanish tortilla is a delicious dish that is served at meal times or as "tapas" (small plates) in bars and restaurants. Enhanced by fire-roasted New Mexico Green chilies, this dish is equally good for lunch, brunch, hors d'oeuvres or appetizers. Serve it with thin slices of Manchego cheese, Monterey Jack or a sharp, aged, white cheddar.

Gorditas

Rebecca Rivera (Louisiana)

4-6 cups Masa flour I use Maseca
warm water to make dough pliable this
varies and must be done by feel.
Canola oil to fry with
1-2 pounds of ground beef browned
and drained
1 medium onion chopped small
6-8 Hatch Green Chiles chopped (the
heat factor is your choice)
1 tsp Mexican Oregano (I grind it up
with my fingers)

1 tsp cumin powder
1 clove garlic minced fine
1 medium white potato cubed
salt and pepper to taste
water to cover the meat mixture
additional cumin and oregano later in the
cooking process.
grated Colby jack cheese about 2 cups

In a heavy skillet brown the ground beef and drain off excess
grease. I rinse mine in hot water to clean off the fat.
With the meat returned to the pan add the next 5 ingredients and
mix them together,add the potato to the mix and add water to cover
the meat mixture and cover with a lid and simmer until potato is
done. This is a binder and adds to the mix.
taste the mixture and season accordingly. Set off to the side.
In a large bowl add the Maseca and warm water until the dough
feels like a moist play dough. Keep water on hand.
Have 2 moist tea towels at the ready and start forming the masa
into discs about 3" in diameter and about 1/4 inch thick.
In heavy skillet (I use my cast iron skillet) heat oil until the a small
piece of dough fries.I fill it between a quarter and half way up the
pan.
Place the masa discs in the hot oil and make all the dough until
finished and place on and under the tea towels.
as soon as the discs turn golden on one side flip them. Cook them
until they are golden.Cook all the discs. Place on a paper towel
lined cookie sheet to drain and cool. Heat oven to 325 degrees and
(I use my cookie cooling racks to set them in and bake them as
well) be ready to cut the shell. Using a sharp knife make an
incision in the side of the shell (with the shell in your hand start at
the top and cut half way down one side and then the other. It will
look like a Pita pocket of sorts. Cut the shell till it makes a pocket.
Fill with the meat mixture and then place in a baking dish or any

type of pan that they can stand up in. Place grated cheese on the meat mixture about a Tablespoon (this again your choice). Cook for about 20-25 minutes or until cheese is melted and the Gorditas are warmed through.
I serve mine with a side of re-fried beans and sopa de fideo. Also a nice Chile con Queso for a dip is excellent.

Personal Notes: I admit I have never written this down I have been taught by the beat and she NEVER wrote anything down. Thank You to my Mother in Law, Josifina. RIP

Pork and Hatch Green Chili Tortas

Michael McGinness (Missouri)

Torta filling:
3 pounds boneless pork butt cut into 2" chunks
1 1/4 cup juiced orange
1 1/4 cup vegetable stock
1 teaspoon sea salt
3 Hatch Green Chilies roasted, skin and seeds removed
4 dried ancho chiles tops and seeds removed
1 1/2 cup of the chile soaking liquid
1/2 cup white onion, roughly chopped
4 garlic cloves, peeled
1/2 cup fresh cilantro leaves
1 teaspoon dried oregano
1/4 teaspoon ground cumin
1/4 teaspoon ground black pepper

2/3 cup cider vinegar vinegar
3 tablespoons vegetable oil
1/4 teaspoon kosher or sea salt

Remainder of ingredients for tortas:
Mexican-style sandwich rolls (bolillos)
Copious amounts of Hatch Green Chilies roasted, skin and seeds removed cut into 1/2" strips
Sliced avocados
Re fried black beans
Pickled red onions
Lime wedges
Queso fresco broken into pieces
Cilantro for garnish

Brown pieces of pork butt in an extended heavy pot. Do not over crowd the pork. After crust has formed on each piece of meat barely cover with the orange juice and vegetable stock. Add salt and set over high heat. Once it comes to a boil, bring the heat down to medium and let is simmer for about 40 minutes, or until most of the liquid has cooked off and the meat is cooked and has rendered most of its fat.

Meanwhile, remove the stems from the chilies. Cut chilies down each side and remove the seeds and veins. Place them in a bowl and cover them with boiling hot water. Let sit and rehydrate for about 15 minutes. Place the chilies and 1 1/2 cups of soaking liquid in a food processor along with the diced Hatch Green Chiles, onion, garlic, parsley, oregano, cumin, black pepper, vinegar, and puree until smooth.

Once the meat is ready, place it in a bowl along with any remaining cooking broth and let cool enough to handle. Shred it with your hands or using two forks.

In the same pot, heat oil over medium heat. Pour in the chile sause and let it season and simmer for 4 to 5 minutes. Toss in the shredded meat along with any of its remaining cooking broth. Sprinkle 1/4 teaspoon salt and let it cook, stirring often, until the meat has absorbed most of the chile sauce, which will have thickened, seasoned and changed color to a much darker tone. It will take about 20 minutes. Taste for salt and add more if need be.

Lightly toast the bolillos in an oven set at 250 F.

To build tortas, slice bolillo and fill with shredded pork and generous amounts of Hatch Green Chile strips!! All other ingredients are optional.

Serve with fire roasted corn on the cob and an ice cold cerveza.

Green Chile Mac and Cheese

Steve Hach (Pennsylvania)

2 lbs. roasted, peeled, seeded, and chopped New Mexican Green Chile that matches a "medium" heat level
3 pounds macaroni, ziti, small penne, etc.
2 sticks plus 2 T butter
1 cup plus 2 T flour
3 T powdered mustard
15 cups milk
2 light American craft beers--Sierra Nevada Pale Ale or similar
1 large yellow onion, finely diced
6 bay leaves
1 T red pepper flakes
6 large eggs, beaten

32 ounces sharp cheddar, shredded
16 ounces extra sharp cheddar, shredded
16 ounces romano cheese, shredded
8 ounces parmesan cheese, shredded
6 teaspoon kosher salt
Fresh black pepper
LARGE roasting pan suitable for 20-25 lbs. Turkey--I use the disposable heavy duty foil ones with the built in handles from the grocery store.

Topping:
6 T butter
2 cups crushed Cheez It crackers

Preheat oven to 350 degrees F.
Boil a very large stock pot of salted water and cook the pasta so that is just al dente or slightly underdone--do NOT cook til it is tender, that is too far.
Drain pasta and place back into large stock pot.
Make a roux using a large sauce pot--melt the butter, then add flour and dry mustard and whisk constantly for 5-7 minutes. Do NOT burn, keep whisking until it is smooth and light tan.
Start adding the milk and stir until it is combined with the roux. If your pot is too small--and it probably is, OOPS--transfer to larger stock pot and add beer, onion, bay leaves, and red pepper flakes.
Simmer sauce for 8-12 minutes.
When sauce has been simmered remove the bay leaves.
Take a small amount, 1 or 2 cups, of the sauce base and slowly add it to the eggs stirring constantly to temper it (you have to do this so it does not turn into scrambled eggs when you add it to the sauce base.)
Pour the tempered egg mixture slowly into the sauce pot while stirring constantly.
Reserve 16 ounces of shredded cheese for topping.
Start adding the remaining shredded cheese to the sauce base while stirring constantly.

Slowly add the rest of the cheese to the sauce base and stir.
Add the diced green chile to the cheese sauce and stir.
Season with salt and pepper.
Slowly pour cheese sauce over pasta in stock pot and carefully combine.
Pour mac and cheese into roasting pan.
Spread reserved shredded cheese over the top.

Make Topping:
Melt butter in pan and toss crushed Cheez It crackers so they are evenly coated.
Top the mac and cheese with the topping mixture. Bake for 30-40 minutes.
Remove from oven and let rest 5-10 minutes before digging in...

Personal Notes: This is a VERY LARGE Portion suitable for a Superbowl Party, Tailgating, the Indy 500, Thanksgiving, etc. To make a more normal size portion, divide all ingredients by 3.

Desserts

SAUCES

WHITE SAUCE	Liquid	Thickening	Fat	Salt
No.1 thin	1 c. milk	1 tbsp. flour	1 tbsp.	1/2 tsp.
No.2 medium	1 c. milk	2 tbsp. flour	1-1/2 tbsp.	1-1/2 tsp.
No.3	1 c. milk	3 tbsp. flour	2 tbsp.	1 tsp.
No.4 thick	1 c. milk	4 tbsp. flour	2-1/2 tbsp.	1 tsp.

Use No.1 sauce for cream soups. Use No.2 sauce for creamed or scalloped dishes or gravy. Use No.3 sauce for soufflés. Use No.4 sauce for croquettes.

VEGETABLE TIMETABLE - MINUTES

VEGETABLE	Boiled	Steamed	Baked
Asparagus Tips	10-15		
Asparagus, tied in bundles	20-30		
Artichokes, French	40	45-60	
Bean, Lima	20-40	60	
Bean, String	15-35	60	
Beets, young with skins on	30	60	70-90
Beets, old	60-120	60-120	
Broccoli, flowerets	5-10		
Broccoli, stems	20-30		
Brussel Sprouts	20-30		
Cabbage, chopped	10-20	25	
Cauliflower, stem down	20-30		
Cauliflower, flowerets	8-10		
Carrots, cut across	20-30	40	
Chard	60-90	90	
Celery, 1-1/2 inch pieces	20-30	45	
Corn, green, tender	5-10	15	20
Corn on the cob	8-10	15	
Eggplant, whole	30	40	45
Marrow	15-40		
Onions	25-40	60	60
Parsnips	25-40	60	60-75
Peas, green	5-15	5-15	
Peppers	20-30	30	30
Potatoes, depending on size	20-40	60	45-60
Potatoes, sweet	40	40	45-60
Scalloped potatoes			60-90
Pumpkin, in cubes	30	45	60
Tomatoes, depending on size	5-15	50	15-20
Turnips, depending on size	25-40		

Green Chile Cheese Pie

Mike (Wyoming)

4 eggs
1/2 c. milk
1 sm. can chopped green chilies,
 drained
1 c. shredded Cheddar cheese

1 c. Monterey Jack cheese, shredded
1/4 tsp. red pepper sauce
9 inch pie crust

Mix all the ingredients and pour into 9 inch pie crust. Bake at 350 degrees for 45 minutes.

Rhubarb, Apple & Green Chile Brown Betty

Alice Shaul Ririe (Oklahoma)

2 cups sliced rhubarb
2 cups sliced apples (peeled or not)
2 or 3 roasted & peeled NM green
 chilies
1 cup sugar
2 tbsp flour
1/2 teaspoon cinnamon

1/2 cup flour
1 cup quick cooking oats
1/2 cup brown sugar
1/3 cup butter, salted
3 tbsp white sugar
1 tsp cinnamon
1/2 cup NM pecans, chopped

TOPPING:

Stir fruit and chile together gently. Mix the sugar and flour and cinnamon in a small bowl Add to the rhubarb mix and let it "juice" up.

Meanwhile stir flour, oats and brown sugar together. Cut in the butter to make a crumbly mixture. Put the fruit in a greased 8" square buttered pan. Top with the oatmeal mixture. Sprinkle with white sugar mixed with cinnamon. Sprinkle pecans on top. Bake in a 350 degree oven for about 50 minutes until bubbly.
Serve warm

Green Chile Pumpkin Pie

Pat Hill (New Mexico)

1/2 cup green chilies, roasted, seeded, peeled and chopped
2 cups pumpkin puree
3 eggs
1 1/2 cups sugar
1/2 cup heavy cream
1 teaspoon cinnamon

1 teaspoon nutmeg
1 teaspoon vanilla
1 Pie crust
Whipped cream
Slivered almonds (if desired)

To roast chilies, place them under broiler flame until skin becomes charred; rotate until all of the skin is blackened. Place chilies in a plastic bag to cool. Once cool, peel off skin and remove stem and seeds. Chop. This step can be done in advance.

Preheat oven to 375 degrees. In a mixing bowl, blend chilies, pumpkin, eggs, sugar, cream, spices and vanilla. Mix well and pour over pie crust.

Bake for 35 minutes, or until pumpkin is firm. Let cool for about 30 minutes.

Top with a dollop of whipped cream and a pinch of roasted almond slivers if desired.

Blackberry Green Chili Key Lime Pie with a Graham Cracker Pinon Crust

Kenn E. Ashe (New Mexico)

Pie filling Ingredients
10 egg yolks, beaten
2 (14 ounce) can sweetened condensed milk
1/2 cup key lime juice
1/2 cup blackberry puree
1 tablespoon green chili/ jalapeno powder
2 (9 inch) prepared pinon-graham cracker crust (Recipe below)

Crust:
2 cups finely crushed graham crackers
1/2 cup of finely chopped pinon nuts
1/3 cup brown sugar
1 tablespoon white sugar
2/3 cup of melted butter

Crust:
Mix first four crust ingredients into a bowl then drizzle melted butter and combine until mix is fully moistened. Press mixture into bottom and sides of 9" pie pan.

Pie Filling:
Preheat oven to 375 degrees F (190 degrees C).
Combine the egg yolks, sweetened condensed milk and lime juice. Mix well. Pour into unbaked graham cracker shell.
Bake in preheated oven for 15 minutes, allow to cool. Top with whipped topping and garnish with jalapeno slices & lime rind if desired.

Apple Cobbler with Green Chile

DeLoris Scherschligt (Oregon)

5-6 Granny Smith or Gala apples, peeled and sliced
2 tablespoons heavy cream
2/3 cup brown sugar, packed
1 tsp cider vinegar
1/4 tsp ground cinnamon
1/4 tsp salt
1/8 tsp allspice
1/8 tsp nutmeg

1 cup granulated sugar
1 1/4 cup flour
1 Tbsp lemon zest, grated
1/8 tsp cinnamon
1/8 tsp nutmeg
3/4 cup butter
1/2 cup Hatch chile peppers, roasted, peeled and chopped

Preheat oven to 375 degrees.

In a large bowl, combine the apples, brown sugar, chilies, vinegar, 1/4 teaspoon cinnamon, 1/4 teaspoon salt, allspice and 1/8 teaspoon nutmeg. Toss until apples are uniformly coated. Spoon into a greased 9x9 baking dish and set aside.

In a medium bowl, combine the sugar, flour, lemon zest, 1/8 teaspoon cinnamon and 1/8 teaspoon nutmeg and mix well. Cut in the butter until crumbly. Stir in the cream. Spread over the apple mixture and press firmly.
Bake at 375 degrees for 45 to 50 minutes or until brown and bubbly.

Chile Berry Thumbprint Cookies

Erin Hurt (Texas)

1 cup all purpose flour	1/2 cup (packed) light brown sugar
1/3 cup cornmeal	1 egg yolk
1/2 tsp cinnamon	1 tsp vanilla
1/8 tsp salt	About 1/4 cup raspberry preserves
1/2 cup (1 stick) unsalted butter, room temperature	About 2 Tbs chopped green chile

Preheat oven to 350 degrees F. Combine flour, cornmeal, cinnamon, and salt in a medium bowl. In another large bowl, using a mixer, beat butter and sugar until fluffy (about 2-3 min.) Mix in egg yolk and vanilla. Fold in dry ingredients.

Form dough into 1 inch balls and place about 1 1/2 inches apart on a ungreased baking sheet (I use parchment paper for easy clean up.) Flatten the ball slightly. Make a depression in the center in the ball with your thumb and fill with a piece of green chile and top with raspberry jam. Bake until bottoms of cookies are golden brown, about 10 min. Cool on rack.

Makes about 2 dozen cookies.

Green Chile Cheesecake

David Leong (New Mexico)

Crust:
Graham cracker crumbs - about 1.5 cups
6 tbsp melted butter
1/4 cup sugar

3/4 cup sugar
1 tsp vanilla
1 cup chopped chile (Place on paper towels to remove as much juice/moisture as possible)

Cheesecake Filling:
3 - 8 oz bricks of cream cheese, room temperature
4 eggs

Topping:
1 cup of sour cream
1 tsp vanilla
3 tbsp sugar

Crust: Mix the crust ingredients and press into greased cheesecake pan.
(Line the outside of the pan with foil because sometime the cakes 'leak').
Bake at 350 for about 10 min; remove and cool while mixing other stuff.

Cheesecake filling: Mix the cream cheese and sugar; add eggs 2 @ a time; stir in vanilla and green chile. Pour into baked crust. Bake at 350 about 55 min - 1 hour. Take out and cool 5 minutes while mixing topping. Loosen sides of pan (after 5 minutes) and then re-close pan.

Topping: Mix topping ingredients; spread over top of cake. Return to 350 oven for 7-9 minutes.

Cool cake for awhile; leave in refrigerator overnight.

Credit goes to my good friend - Sherri Huffman

Hatch Green Chile Mexican Chocolate Mousse (Top 10 Grand Prize Winner)

Elaine Gonzalez (Arizona)

3 mild or medium roasted, seeded and peeled Hatch green chiles
1/2 round Nestle Abuelita hot chocolate tablet
1 square dark chocolate from your favorite chocolate brand. I used Godiva 72% Cacao.
1/2 cup water, divided
3 egg yolks

2 tbsp sugar
2 tbsp butter. No substitutions!
1 1/4 cup heavy cream
1/2 packet unflavored gelatin
1/4 tsp vanilla extract

1. "Toast" your green chiles in the 2 tbsp butter, remove chiles and set them aside to cool. After they have cooled a bit, chop them into 1/4 inch or smaller pieces.
2. In a double boiler, add 1/4 cup water, the butter from toasting your chiles and the chocolates. Stir and melt, takes about 6-8 minutes. Let it cool for about 5-10 minutes. You don't want it to be so hot that it cooks your eggs or so cool that it starts to harden.
3. While your chocolate mixture is melting in double boiler, use mixer to whip heavy cream into whipped cream: Pour heavy cream in mixer bowl, add 1/2 small packet of unflavored gelatin and the vanilla. Set to medium-high speed and let the cream fluff up.
4. In a small heavy-bottomed sauce pan, add the 3 egg yolks, sugar and the rest of the water (1/4 cup). Whisk together on low heat until mixture reaches about 160 degrees F. Stir while it is heating up. This should take only 3 or so minutes. Don't leave it on the heat! Your eggs will scramble!
5. Add ice to a big enough bowl to fit your small sauce pan. Put your sauce pan with egg mixture in the bowl of ice to cool and whisk in the chocolate mixture. Stir in your chopped green chiles, then, when mixture is cool, fold in the whipped cream.
6. Spoon mousse into serving cups and refrigerate until set. Garnish with extra whipped cream. Or better yet, make a lime whipped cream!!!

Green Chili Nut Chocolate Truffles

Cathleen Krepps (New Mexico)

1/2 cup whole almonds
1 1/2 cups each of dried fruit :cherries, cranberries, and apricots
1 tbsp Honey
1 tbsp fresh, roasted green chili, drained well

1/4 cup roasted almond butter
dried spices: ginger, Biad dried green chili powder, cinnamon, salt
8 oz dark Chocolate chopped into pieces

Place 1/2 cup whole almonds in dry skillet over medium-high heat, stirring until fragrant -- about 5 minutes. Remove from heat and take out of pan to cool then chop and place in bowl.

Chop dried fruit into small pieces and add to nuts.

Mix 1 tsp cinnamon, 1/2 tsp Biad Mild Green chili powder, 1/8 tsp salt and 1/2 tsp ground ginger. This is a very forgiving recipe, so you can add more spices to your taste. Sprinkle over dried fruit and nuts then mix.

Mix in:
1 tbsp well drained, chopped, roasted, mild, green chile
1 tbsp Honey
1/4 cup roasted almond butter
Mix well by hand

Place parchment paper on cookie sheets. Roll teaspoons of mixture with your hands into small balls and place onto parchment paper. Place in refrigerator until ready to dip into chocolate.

Melt chocolate in double boiler, or metal bowl set over pan of simmering water. Stir constantly with spatula, not wooden spoon. Do not let any water get into chocolate. When chocolate is melted, remove from pan and place on counter on a towel. If chocolate begins to harden, place over hot water again and stir until melted.

Roll the fruit chile nut balls in chocolate one at a time, and place back on cookie sheet. (You can also roast additional almonds and chop, and roll the truffles in the nuts right after dipping in chocolate if you like or roll in cocoanut.) Place fruit balls on cookie sheets and put in refrigerator till set.

Store in airtight container, in refrigerator until ready to serve.

Sinfully Spicy Apple Pie (Top 10 Grand Prize Winner)
Jordan Calaway (California)

Crust
2 1/2 cups unbleached all purpose
  flour
3 tsp sugar
1/2 tsp cinnamon
1/2 pound butter
1/2 cup iced chile juice (reserved from
  steeping or frozen chile)(iced water
  can be substituted)
2 cups shredded Tillamook sharp
  cheddar cheese

Filling
10 Granny Smith Green Apples (2.5
  pounds) Peeled, cored and sliced

2 cups Big Jim Green Chile (Roasted,
  peeled, chopped)
1 1/2 cup sugar
1 1/2 tsp cinnamon
1/4 cup chile juice (reserved from
  steeping or frozen chile)(water can be
substituted)
1/2 cup flour
4 ounces butter
2 Tbsp milk
sugar and cinnamon for sprinkling
9.5" Pyrex pie pan

Warning- This pie IS addictive and you will be enslaved to the great sweet heat! Try at your own risk of never eating a plain apple pie again.

Crust-
Chop butter into 1/4" cubes and keep cold in refrigerator. Food process all dry ingredients until thoroughly mixed. Fold in butter until mixture resembles crumbs (pea size) Add cold chile juice. Mix in shredded cheese until mixture starts to form large clump. (20 seconds or so). Divide dough in half and press into 4" disk. Place on greased plate, cover and refrigerate.

Filling-
Combine apples, sugar, flour, chile, cinnamon, butter and chile

juice in bowl and mix. Let rest in refrigerator for a minimum 30 minutes

Dough-
Roll out crust 1" bigger then upside down 9.5" pie pan. Grease pan and lightly flower. Place bottom crust in pie pan allowing excess to hang over the rim and lightly flower. Roll out top crust. Pour apple mixture into pie pan and place top crust. Pinch together top and bottom crusts and roll up (picture out side of a pizza crust).
With a the tines of a fork, poke holes for steam venting. Place pie in refrigerator for 15 minutes. Pre heat oven to 350 degrees. Brush crust with milk and sprinkle cinnamon and sugar on top. Place on middle rack for 60 minutes or until crust turns dark golden brown.
Allow to cool for 20 minutes. Serve warm and enjoy! Warning you may want to eat two pieces....I won't tell

Personal Notes: Total Time: 2 hours 15 minutes
Prep: 30 minutes
Inactive: 45 minutes
Cook: 60 minutes

Notes

Notes

Index of Recipes

Order Form

To order additional copies of:

Biad Chili Tough Book of Green Chile Recipes

Please contact:

Biad Chili Products
575-525-0034
cbiad@biadchili.com
Visit us: www.BiadChili.com
Like us: www.facebook.com/
HatchGreenChile.com

To begin your own family Cookbook Project or to
create a cookbook as part of a fundraiser, visit
www.familycookbookproject.com